TEACHING AND LEARNING WITH TECHNOLOGY

Teaching and Learning with Technology sets out key principles for digital learning underpinned by research evidence. It explores the ways in which technology can help teachers to achieve their goals and support good pedagogy and offers practical strategies for using technology when planning and delivering effective lessons.

Drawing on examples from across the curriculum and highlighting a wide range of key technologies, chapters cover:

- Live remote teaching
- Delivering content and instruction
- Using technology to assess learning
- Alternative learning platforms
- Ensuring accessibility and personalising learning
- E-safety, safeguarding and legal compliance
- Implementing and managing change in digital education

Written by a leading expert in digital education and filled with easy-to-implement tips, this book is an essential guide for all teachers delivering lessons online.

Matt Jarvis is a Chartered Psychologist, award-winning Certified Learning Technologist and teacher with over 25 years of experience in education and working with private training providers. He currently leads learning technology and innovation for a large social justice and education charity, where he has managed the transition to digital education.

TEACHING AND LEARNING WITH TECHNOLOGY

How to Make E-Learning Work for You and Your Learners

Matt Jarvis

LONDON AND NEW YORK

Designed cover image: © Getty Images

First published 2023
by Routledge
4 Park Square, Milton Park, Abingdon, Oxon OX14 4RN

and by Routledge
605 Third Avenue, New York, NY 10158

Routledge is an imprint of the Taylor & Francis Group, an informa business

© 2023 Matt Jarvis

All rights reserved. No part of this book may be reprinted or reproduced or utilised in any form or by any electronic, mechanical, or other means, now known or hereafter invented, including photocopying and recording, or in any information storage or retrieval system, without permission in writing from the publishers.

Trademark notice: Product or corporate names may be trademarks or registered trademarks, and are used only for identification and explanation without intent to infringe.

The word Moodle and associated Moodle logos are trademarks or registered trademarks of Moodle Pty Ltd or its related affiliates.

British Library Cataloguing-in-Publication Data
A catalogue record for this book is available from the British Library

Library of Congress Cataloging-in-Publication Data
Names: Jarvis, Matt, 1966- author.
Title: Teaching and learning with technology : how to make E-learning work for you and your learners / Matt Jarvis.
Description: Abingdon, Oxon ; New York, NY : Routledge, 2023. | Includes bibliographical references and index.
Identifiers: LCCN 2022041190 (print) | LCCN 2022041191 (ebook) | ISBN 9781032210438 (hardback) | ISBN 9781032210445 (paperback) | ISBN 9781003266471 (ebook)
Subjects: LCSH: Web-based instruction. | Internet in education. | Educational technology.
Classification: LCC LB1044.87 .J36 2023 (print) | LCC LB1044.87 (ebook) | DDC 371.33/44678--dc23/eng/20221021
LC record available at https://lccn.loc.gov/2022041190
LC ebook record available at https://lccn.loc.gov/2022041191

ISBN: 978-1-032-21043-8 (hbk)
ISBN: 978-1-032-21044-5 (pbk)
ISBN: 978-1-003-26647-1 (ebk)

DOI: 10.4324/9781003266471

Typeset in Interstate
by SPi Technologies India Pvt Ltd (Straive)

CONTENTS

Preface	vii
1 Introduction	1
Learning from history	1
Living after interesting times	3
The digital divide	4
What makes (digital) learning effective?	4
Three genuinely useful theories	6
2 Presenting content for knowledge transfer	11
Linear presentation tools: PowerPoint, Google Slides and Impress	11
Alternatives to traditional presenters	16
Multimedia	20
Working with audio	23
E-books	25
3 Digital assessment	29
A quick recap on assessment	29
Baseline assessment	30
Formative assessment	32
Quiz tools	38
Assignment tools	39
Gamification	42
Using technology to prepare for summative assessment	44
4 Digital learning platforms	47
Base platforms, walled gardens and integrations	48
Cloud-based office environments	48
External non-office platforms	52
Virtual Learning Environments	53
VLE design: the example of Moodle	54
5 Remote teaching	60
Synchronous, asynchronous and blended lessons	60
Technology for remote teaching	63
Tools and techniques to aid live instruction	68

	Remote teaching lifehacks	74
	Tricky remote teaching scenarios	78

6 Keeping digital education legal, accessible and safe — 80
Digital education and law — 80
Data protection — 80
Accessibility — 83
Copyright — 86
E-safety — 87

7 Digital leadership and change — 96
Digital leadership — 96
Understanding your organisation — 98
Your digital development plan — 102
Understanding and planning for change — 104
Using the SAMR model to evaluate a proposed change — 104
Co-design: a wraparound model for planning and implementing change — 107
Implementing and anchoring change — 110

Glossary — 113
Appendix: Brief accessibility audit — 123
Index — 127

PREFACE

Who and what is this book for?

This book is intended as a practical guide for teachers and anyone else involved in digital education – including teachers, managers, teaching assistants, mentors and home-schooling parents. I don't assume any prior knowledge of educational technology (ed tech) or e-learning practices, although I do assume that you have access to a computer and an Internet connection and that you have the basic IT skills to open a browser.

I didn't want to write an instruction manual for using one or more particular applications – there are plenty of those about already, and no book is ever going to do that as well as a decent YouTube channel. However, neither is this an academic textbook – hence the minimal referencing and theory. I wanted this to be a practical guide to what you can (and sometimes what you can't) do with technology as a teacher or school or college manager tasked with planning and implementing technology, why you might want to do particular stuff and what applications will get you closer to where you want to be.

I bring a slightly unusual perspective to all this in that I'm a Certified Learning Technologist and JISC-accredited Digital Leader, a Chartered Psychologist and a qualified teacher with 25 years of classroom experience. This means that I know both the current technologies and the theory that has informed their design and application. But, crucially, I also know what real life is like at the chalkface. I'll try to be as honest and realistic as possible about how long stuff takes to prepare, who it may not appeal to and what can go wrong.

The philosophy of this book

All teachers tread a tricky line between being wanting to identify as autonomous reflective professionals on one hand and daily survival as overstretched pragmatists on the other. Some readers will lean towards wanting to make informed decisions, while others will just want to know what to do. No book will get the balance right for everyone, but for what it's worth, here are the principles I've kept in mind when choosing what to write about and offering advice.

- *Self-determination*: We are all more motivated when we feel like we are making our own choices. Wherever possible, I've tried to offer you choices and to explain the pros and cons of each option.

- *Evidence-base*: This one comes riddled with provisos, because we are dealing with a field that changes too rapidly for the cycle of academic research and publication to keep pace, and because evidence gathered in one context may not generalise well to others. Where possible, though, I have been broadly informed by research.
- *Everyone matters*: This is more than a statement of the bleeding obvious. We work in a pressured and politicised system, where it's normal to prioritise the needs of one group at the expense of another. I've tried to offer solutions with wide benefits, or at least make it explicit where a particular group of students is likely to suffer from a policy or strategy. But I also think it's important to consider the implications of digital practices for the workload and stress experienced by teachers and other staff.
- *Balancing the art and science of pedagogy*: I can tell you about applications, offer tips for using them and tell you what research suggests should work – that's the science bit. BUT the nuances of tweaking your practice to the needs of individuals, groups and subjects, and the processes of reflecting on and adapting your practice will always be an art, and on that *you* are the expert, even if you don't feel like one the first time you try a new technology.
- *Legal compliance and Ofsted-friendly practice*: I deliberately left the Killjoy Principle until last, as I don't want to dampen anyone's creativity, but you won't want your hard work to be spoiled by a GDPR breach or by unknowingly going against DfE guidance and being pulled up for it come next inspection.

Being pedagogy-led and tech-enabled

If there's one thing I can get you thinking about at the outset that will make a difference as to how useful this book or any other on e-learning and ed tech becomes, it's this: Try to plan from the point of what you'd like to be able to do, *not* what a particular application can easily do or what it looks like it should be used for. In other words, set your goals according to principles of good pedagogy and use the technology to enable you to achieve these goals.

A common alternative approach – and a mistake, in my opinion – is to start by looking at what your chosen platform looks like and how it looks like it should be used. You should be thinking about choosing a platform or platforms only in the light of what you want to achieve. And as an aside, all platforms can work together or in parallel, so as a school or college, you *don't* have to choose a single platform and stick rigidly to it. A *massive* pet hate of mine is hearing 'we can't do that, we're a Google school' or 'but we're committed to Microsoft solutions.' There is, of course, nothing wrong with those platforms, but you – either individually or as a school or college community – should be in control of what you can and can't do, and the only limitations (excepting cost) should be what works for you and your students. Anything else is the tail wagging the dog.

There is always (okay, *almost* always) a way to do what you would like, and often you'll be surprised at how little it costs or how little inconvenience it entails. There are sometimes very good reasons to keep things simple (or at least to start simple and upgrade your capabilities with caution), but that should be your informed and planned choice.

Balancing generic and subject-specific practice

The distinction between generic and subject-specific pedagogy has been around since the 1980s, but it has recently been enshrined in the 2018 Ofsted review of evidence-supported practice. Different subjects have their own pedagogical needs, and communities of subject teachers have evolved distinct cultures, practices and identities. So, if you are an English teacher, you probably won't be impressed by true/false or multiple-choice quizzes, and if you've been around a while, you will probably have experienced e-learning evangelists trying to push them on you!

There is, however, technology that you might like better. For example, you might be more impressed by collaborative annotation, writing frames with interactive prompts, debating or multimedia diarising tools or perhaps audio-based quiz tools that can create on-line spelling tests. It is therefore worth looking beyond the headline applications and platforms to find the tools that will enable the pedagogy you value. I will make occasional suggestions for subject-specific use of tools and use examples from different subjects, but the main point is that whatever you teach, you will find something useful here but also many things that don't work for you. Rather than let others prescribe what ed tech you should use, I would suggest taking the bull by the horns and find some tools that fit with what you want to do.

1 Introduction

By the end of this chapter, I hope you will be able to:

- Learn lessons from previous failures in the development of ed tech and e-learning
- Distinguish between synchronous and asynchronous delivery, activities and lessons, and appreciate the role of each
- Identify some general principles of effective teaching and learning
- Use a small number of carefully chosen theories to make sense of and plan digital practice

If you are itching to get on with planning and delivering, you might want to skip this chapter – although I would recommend that you come back to it when you have more time. After this I will get entirely practical (promise!). This chapter, though, is for those who like to take a step back and reflect on where we are, how we got here and why stuff is or isn't working for us. It is also a chance to ground yourself in a bit of history, policy, pedagogy and psychology.

The hectic pace of teaching means that inevitably we often end up planning for the next day, and we tend to frame our planning in the mechanical processes of how to deliver a particular lesson to a particular group. For some at least, the way off that treadmill is to take a step back and use the lessons of history, psychological theory and shared pedagogical practice to equip us to work smarter rather than harder.

Learning from history

E-Learning and educational technology have a chequered history of modest successes, frequent failure and unintended consequences. This is not to insult anyone or diminish their contributions – I'm absolutely one of the people that have repeatedly got excited about new technology, rolled it out and seen it either roundly ignored or adopted but with unanticipated and sometimes unwelcome results! It has proved surprisingly tricky to tell when a new piece of kit will catch on or how it will be used on the ground.

DOI: 10.4324/9781003266471-1

2 Introduction

As philosopher George Santayana (1863-1952) famously said, "Those who cannot remember the past are condemned to repeat it." We can't anticipate everything, but we can learn lessons from experience. Here are some important lessons:

1. *Focus on what you want to achieve with a particular application, not what it looks like it's meant to be used for.* So, for example, PowerPoint and similar presentation applications look like tools for delivering endless bullet points and talking over them, and when PowerPoint hit education in the 1990s, that's exactly how (by and large) it was used. It shouldn't be a surprise – with the benefit of hindsight, of course – that the impact on learning was not initially positive. Of course, there are much better ways to use presentation tools – these are discussed in detail in Chapter 3.
2. *Don't be surprised when an application that changes how you work fails to excite your students.* When Virtual Learning Environments like Moodle became a thing in the 2000s, many teachers and Learning Technologists wondered why their students were not more excited. However – and again, hindsight is perfect – from the student perspective there was nothing remotely exciting about a repository of the presentations they had already seen and documents they had already read. Don't get me wrong, Moodle is awesome, and I strongly believe you should all have access to one, but it takes significant expertise and effort to set up its full functionality and work with teachers to exploit its potential. I will try to do some of this work for you in Chapter 4.
3. *There are generational differences in how students respond to technology.* So-called 'digital natives' are not necessarily better with technology *per se* than older folks, but they do tend to respond to it *differently*, and it's important to consider their responses to what you do. To my generation, who are used to thinking in structural, almost geographical terms about *where* to find *things* on *sites*, something like the Google Suite interface can seem unintuitive, however brilliantly each application within it is thought out. To younger people, who intuitively think as much in terms of tech *function* as structure, this is simply not an issue. You don't always need to change what you do according to the whims of your students. In fact, their ability to adapt to a range of technology design is just the kind of transferable skill that will help futureproof their employability. If, however, you aren't getting the engagement you anticipated, this may be an avenue to investigate.
4. *No digital experiences replicate on a like-for-like basis the experiences that students and teachers have in the classroom.* This one is a recent lesson from the Covid lockdowns. You can – to some extent – simulate classroom experiences in virtual space, but it won't be the same. How much that matters and whether it's a bad thing depends on what you are trying to achieve and with whom. Traditionally, we have used technology to enhance the experience of learning in or around a conventional classroom so that many of students' learning and social-emotional needs have been met outside the technology domain. Live remote teaching is a very different beast, and it is hard to sustain students' interest, engagement and positivity over an extended period without some face-to-face contact. If you are engaged in remote teaching, don't exhaust yourself trying or beat yourself up for struggling with this. It is probably more productive to set modest goals and capitalise on the opportunity to get students working more independently.

Living after interesting times

For anyone involved with education, recent times have been 'interesting,' both literally and sometimes in the sense of the (probably apocryphal) 'may you live in interesting times' curse! Covid-19 changed everything in digital education, although this change is ongoing. On one hand the whole world of education, from very young children through teachers and managers up to the ministerial level, now know something about education technology and appreciate its importance. On the other hand, we are now operating in the aftermath of the growth of very particular kinds of technology tailored to the need to deliver live, remote teaching; what kinds of tech the typical teacher and student will need in the future is much less certain.

Scientists tell us that there will be more pandemics, and there may be other scenarios in which we rely again on remote teaching. If we are to prepare for all the likely scenarios facing us, then our digital pedagogy needs to be broad and flexible enough to cope with a range of scenarios:

- Technology-enhanced conventional classroom teaching, using a range of applications to deliver, assess and monitor progress; and additional tools to support homework, flipped learning, portfolio building and exam preparation
- Blended learning involving reduced face-to-face contact, supplemented by more independent digital learning
- Remote digital teaching, in which all or most contact between teacher and learner is mediated by technology
- Hybrid classrooms in which some students are physically present whilst others are accessing remotely

'Synchronous' and 'asynchronous' is now a thing!

Before 2020, pretty much, only Learning Technologists talked about synchronous and asynchronous use of technology. In terms of remote delivery, that distinction is arguably the key to understanding successful digital learning and planning a meaningful and sustainable pedagogy. Synchronous technology is not always well understood: Life always happens in real time, and here we are really talking about teaching activities that involve real-time *communication*. By contrast, in asynchronous teaching we are not communicating in real time; we might leave instructions for a task or sequence of tasks, or we might leave students for a time to get on with a project and pick up on how they are getting on later. The same lessons can involve synchronous and asynchronous elements. Although the synchronous–asynchronous distinction came to the fore during lockdown, it is also key to understanding different activities in the conventional classroom.

More about synchronous and asynchronous tools, activities and lessons can be found in Chapters 2 and 3. My point for now is that in the context of the necessity for remote teaching and the novelty of shiny new tools like MS Teams and Google Meet schools, colleges and individual teachers have shifted away from asynchronous environments to their cost. Asynchronous technology, including that shared in a partially synchronous lesson, allows students to learn actively and independently at their own pace and offers opportunities to reflect, make choices and think deeply.

The digital divide

With the best will in the world, education discriminates, and reliance on any kind of technology outside the physical classroom, in which you have *some* ability to intervene to compensate for disadvantage, may make this worse. This applies to homework, flipped learning and exam prep in the context of conventional teaching as much as blended and remote teaching. Consider the following:

- Students living in poverty are likely to have less access to appropriate hardware and connectivity. Where schools and colleges are open, we can partly compensate for this by facilitating independent study and providing the necessary technology in the building. However, where we can't facilitate that, poor students become *really* disadvantaged, as they don't have access to the equipment and physical environment of the school or college.
- Nor is it simply a question of money and equipment. Many young people simply don't have access to a quiet space to study in, or it may be available at particular times that don't fit around a remote delivery timetable or homework strategy. Some families – for a whole variety of reasons mainly not of their own making – are not supportive of formal education, and this puts their children at a motivational disadvantage even when they have suitable devices and connections.
- Young people living with food and fuel poverty, or abuse or the fear of it, have more pressing concerns than completing homework or attending remote lessons. It is entirely sensible that they are preoccupied with their physical and safety needs first. As education professionals, of course, *we* know that education provides reliable long-term routes out of that situation, but we must appreciate that it will rarely be the immediate priority of the student.
- To make things worse, sources of disadvantage do not operate in isolation but intersect. A girl from a family living in poverty and facing the stress of racism, whose family values do not prioritise education or women's careers, who has caring responsibilities for other family members and therefore less freedom to participate in after-school classes, may be *further* disadvantaged by unplanned reliance on flipped and independent learning.

This is not meant to depress you or make you feel responsible for solving all society's problems. It's just worth thinking about how your plans for digital learning, whether they focus on bring-your-own-device learning, remote teaching, flipped learning or plain old-fashioned homework, will look very different from the perspective of different students. Something as simple as letting students use the computers in your classroom at lunchtime, encouraging them to use a homework club or offering recorded remote lessons for those who cannot access them live can help mitigate disadvantage. Your students won't think of you in ten years and reminisce about how skilfully you used Google Classroom hacks, but they *will* remember you noticing their needs and providing bespoke help.

What makes (digital) learning effective?

This is a real back-to-basics question, but one that can easily get lost as we focus on mastering the mechanics of new technologies. Digital learning is learning, just mediated by technology. All the same principles that underlie effective conventional learning in a physical classroom still apply, even though how we achieve them may differ. There are a range of published taxonomies of what makes teaching and/or learning effective, so this is not definitive, but I have found these useful:

- Learning should (generally) be an active process
- Learning should (generally) be an interactive process
- Learning for exam-based assessment should be memorable
- Learning should be accessible to all and personalised to the needs of the individual

We can pick all these up in detail in later chapters, but here is a summary.

Active learning

Generally, learning should be an active process rather than a passive one, BUT there are a couple of huge provisos to this. First, the 'active' in active learning should refer to mental activity, not to the superficial appearance of active behaviour. There is an art to planning lessons rich in mental activity, and it depends on knowing your students. So, a teacher-led class discussion is not necessarily passive, though it may become so – you know better than anyone else how many of your students will stay engaged in discussion and for how long. On the other hand, although project-based learning *sounds* active, participating in an unstructured project is not necessarily a particularly active process, as it provides an easy opportunity for less motivated individuals to disengage (Ofsted, 2018). Again, you know better than anyone else whether your students engage well with projects, and you know what kind of cognitive activation – recap quizzes, debates etc. – work for them. Planning and managing remote lessons that keep students engaged is harder, and you may have to modify your expectations.

The second proviso is that there *are* (contrary to conventional wisdom) learning strategies that are not particularly active in a behavioural or cognitive sense, but nonetheless lead to learning. So, pushing out regular small chunks of information (the simplest form of microlearning) leads to a drip-feeding effect in which a modest volume of information is absorbed over time. This can be understood in terms of cognitive load (described in the 'Cognitive load theory' section in this chapter, p. 8) and is discussed further in later chapters.

Interactive learning

We are a social species, and we are designed to do most things better with other people. Learning is no exception and, as a broad rule, social interaction enhances learning, provided it is task-relevant interaction. In the physical classroom, interaction can take place between students, e.g. in the form of group work, peer tutoring and peer marking, and between teacher and learner, for example through tutorials, feedback and whole-class interactive discussions. All of these interactions can be to some extent simulated in digital contexts, where there is also the potential for interaction with software and even artificial intelligences. We pick up the theme of interaction in Chapters 2 and 5.

Memorable learning

Clearly, active and interactive learning help when it comes to good retention of information. However, when it comes preparing for exam-based assessment there are a number of additional tools and planning hacks that you can use to boost students' memory. We will explore this in detail in Chapter 4.

Personalised learning

There are three related ideas here:

- Accessibility refers to whether resources and activities are suitable for diverse students with a range of sensory, physical and cognitive abilities and disabilities.
- Differentiation used to mean labelling students by ability and planning to cater to these abilities. Increasingly, the term is now used to mean (and is being replaced by) *adapting* what we do in the light of student progress – including in real time within lessons, modifying explanations, feedback and upcoming tasks in the light of current progress. Adaptive technology provides this in the context of e-learning.
- Personalisation is the broadest term, referring to all the ways we can tailor the experience of learning to the needs and preferences of the individual. This can include not only meeting their accessibility needs, but also adapting activities according to progress and adopting different delivery methods according to student circumstances and preferences – for example, offering asynchronous alternatives to live lessons.

Personalising the student experience of digital learning is both science and art. There is, for example, a science to knowing about the range of digital accessibility aids and what they can do to support different needs. The interpersonal process of working with the individual to see what works *for them* is an art and is an important aspect of digital pedagogy.

> **Top tech tip:** If you really want to meet the individual needs of your students, consider accessibility, differentiation, adaptation and personalisation. There may well be a combination of factors that revolutionises the experience of education for students, but it will be highly individual. The more factors you consider as you work with a student, the better the chance you have of discovering what works for them.

Three genuinely useful theories

Whole books much larger than this one can and have been written about psychological theory and education. All approaches to teaching are either based on a theory of learning or have been justified and explained in their light. I'm well aware that most teachers are not interested in theory; nonetheless, I will offer accounts of three theories that I have found absolutely key to my understanding of particular aspects of human nature in the context of digital education. They may or may not resonate similarly with you.

Affordances: why people use technology wrong

Psychologist J. J. Gibson put forward the radical theory of direct visual perception. The central idea is that, instead of looking at something and deciding what it is and what it is for based on a memory search and comparison with different things we have seen in the past, we work out what it is and what to do with it by its appearance. So, we recognise a chair not by comparing it to all the objects we've seen before, but because it looks like something to sit on. To use Gibson's term, it *affords* sitting.

An object's affordances are the relationships between its potential and apparent uses. Most Learning Technologists have focused on potential and speak of affordances as the sum of what a tool can be used for. I'm approaching affordances slightly differently and returning to Gibson's central idea that what a tool looks like determines what it appears to be for and how it should be used. The classic example of how affordances influence our behaviour are door handles. In this example, the handles clearly look like they are meant to be pulled – i.e., they *afford* pulling. The push sign could be in 10-foot-high letters of blood; people will still pull them!

The same principle of affordances can be applied to understanding why people use software the way they do. For example:

- PowerPoint *affords* bullet points, so people tend to overuse bullets
- Moodle *affords* the 'scroll of death,' in which huge numbers of files are hung in a column
- Zoom *affords* talking, so teachers tend to talk too much when remote teaching

Figure 1.1 In spite of the sign, this door affords pulling so people pull rather than push it.
Source: Pixabay 5619110.

> **Top tech tip**: Once you know about affordances, you have a powerful thinking tool with which you can decide whether your first thought about how to plan a presentation slide, VLE page or remote lesson is actually the right one. Often it won't be. So, every time you approach one of these tasks, consciously consider the range of alternative formats you could employ.

Self-determination theory: why we tend to prefer our own technology choices

This one may resonate particularly with school and college leaders, who might have had the embarrassing experience of showing a policy saying one thing to an inspector and being asked why they have just observed a lesson in which something entirely different took place! According to Edward Deci and Richard Ryan, we are motivated by three basic psychological needs:

- *Autonomy*: We like to believe that we are freely making our own choices
- *Competence*: We like to believe that we are good at tasks
- *Relatedness*: We seek social interaction, attachment and belonging to groups

According to SDT, these three factors affect our intrinsic motivation, i.e. motivation that comes from within as opposed to external motivation in the form of reward and punishment. Self-determination theory predicts that the more autonomous, competent and related we are in relation to aspects of our work, the harder we will work at them. If you work at a school that is committed, let's say to Microsoft technology when you prefer Google, your intrinsic motivation to work with that technology is likely to be low. You haven't been able to make your own choice, and although you can become competent, you aren't at first; and anyway, it won't be the competence you really wanted to develop. You might comply because of extrinsic factors like fear of punishment, but this is usually a less powerful motivator than intrinsic motivation.

> **Top tech tip**: If you shape policy, unless there are compelling reasons to restrict teachers' choices of technology, give them some options and encourage sharing of teacher-led practice – *even when you are convinced your ideas are better*. A standardised approach might look neat in a policy document, but it might risk undermining teacher motivation – and a significant minority won't comply anyway. Teachers working hard using what you see as a less efficient strategy will probably still achieve more than teachers implementing your preferred approach half-heartedly. If you are the teacher feeling a bit hemmed in by an institutional policy, make a case for broadening it out.

Cognitive load theory: using the science of human memory to optimise learning

Cognitive load theory (CLT) explains the relationship between learning in the context of education and the workings of human memory. In particular, it is concerned with the properties of short-term or working memory and how it interacts with long-term memory. Working memory is the system we use when we are perceiving and thinking about something. It has separate sub-systems for handling information in different forms (e.g. audio and visual) and draws on information from the senses and long-term memory.

Crucially, working memory has a limited capacity that can be overloaded, reducing the success of learning. However, not all additional tasks related to incoming information reduce learning because they can lead to additional processing of the information that makes transfer to long-term memory more likely – i.e. they increase the success of learning. John Sweller, the originator of CLT, distinguishes between three types of cognitive load:

- *Intrinsic cognitive load*: Every fact we present students with, every task we ask them to complete and every skill we expect them to master has an intrinsic cognitive load. To put it another way, some things are just harder to learn than others. Although intrinsic cognitive load is not itself changeable, we can sometimes ease the difficulty of taking on a new idea, e.g. by using animation on a presentation to add each facet of the idea one at a time.
- *Extraneous cognitive load*: Any additional sources of information we have to process while simultaneously processing the fact, task or skill reduce the processing capacity available to cope with its intrinsic cognitive load. This is much more under our control as teachers and content developers. In fact, the basic strategies based on CLT are all about reducing extraneous cognitive load. When we reduce the number of words on a slide, remove unnecessary animation and audio, simplify the appearance of a web page or spread information across two processing channels by narrating a diagram instead of adding written labels, we are reducing extraneous cognitive load. Reducing sentence length and removing unfamiliar words do much the same thing. Teachers often work to reduce extraneous cognitive load intuitively, for example when we advise students not to listen to music or chat whilst revising.
- *Germane cognitive load*: Some elements of a learning task can benefit learning in spite of adding to cognitive load. This is because they involve the kind of intensive cognitive processing that helps to build schemas, knowledge structures in long-term memory, or strengthens pathways between working memory and schemas so that it becomes easier to retrieve information. Worked examples are the classic example of tasks designed to increase germane cognitive load. Cognitive activation in the form of tasks that get students to think deeply increases germane load as does cognitive effort, for example, created by adding time pressure, which increases alertness and hence the ability to allocate greater working memory capacity.

Just to complicate things slightly, CLT also references the expertise reversal effect, in which what is germane for a novice learner becomes extraneous for an expert. This means that different lesson formats and tasks might impact differently on different students. There are numerous ways in which we can manipulate extraneous and germane cognitive load, and we will look at these particularly in Chapters 2 and 3.

Just to tease you with one example of expertise reversal in the use of technology, talking over a presentation is likely to add germane cognitive load for students new to a topic, as the dual channels of information input through working memory provide more than one route to schema formation. However, once students are familiar with the topic, you are likely to find that this no longer helps.

Further information

There has been a lot of discussion recently around how to balance synchronous and asynchronous uses of technology. The free Open University course 'Take your teaching online' (https://www.open.edu/openlearn/education-development/education/take-your-teaching-online/content-section-overview?active-tab=content-tab) deals with synchronous and asynchronous teaching as do a range of modules from the Education & Training Foundation (e.g. 'Asynchronous learning & teaching and Collaborating synchronously with learners' – https://enhance.etfoundation.co.uk/explore/synchronous).

The angle on affordances that I have focused on is unusual, so I don't really recommend casual reading around it, although if you are particularly interested, see Hammond's (2010) paper (https://wrap.warwick.ac.uk/34602/). For something on self-determination theory in the context of management you might like to try these: Rigby and Ryan (2018), (https://institute.welcoa.org/wp/wp-content/uploads/2019/09/Rigby-Ryan-selfdetermination-theory-hr.pdf) and Stone, Deci and Ryan (2008) (https://selfdeterminationtheory.org/SDT/documents/2009_StoneDeciRyan_JGM.pdf).

For more on cognitive load, try Enser (2019) for an introduction (https://www.tes.com/news/how-useful-cognitive-load-theory-teachers), and Castro-Alonso and Koning (2020) for something more advanced (https://repositorio.uchile.cl/bitstream/handle/2250/177891/Latest-trends.pdf?sequence=1).

2 Presenting content for knowledge transfer

From PowerPoint to interactive multimedia

By the end of this chapter, I hope you will be able to:

- Put together more engaging presentations using conventional presentation software
- Use a range of alternative presentation software including Prezi, Slides and Emaze
- Understand the benefits of interactivity in presentations, and develop interactive presentations using H5P/Lumi
- Use audio and video to convey information, including screencasting and podcasting
- Add interactivity to video material using H5P/Lumi
- Make conventional and interactive multimedia e-books and deploy them effectively

Whether you are presenting in real time or handing over a presentation to students, and whether your delivery is in a physical classroom, online or a blend of the two, presenting information, tasks and instructions to your students is fundamental to teaching. There is a huge choice in the tools you can use for this, and, more importantly, a range of things to consider in how and when you use them. Let's start with the humble PowerPoint and its alternatives.

Linear presentation tools: PowerPoint, Google Slides and Impress

Linear presentations are those that you proceed through in a single predetermined sequence of slides. Actually, any presentation tool can make linear presentations, and no tool confines you to linear presentations alone. However, tools like PowerPoint and Google Slides *look* like sequential presenters and default to producing sequential slides unless you make a conscious effort to use them differently, so in practice we can think of them as linear presenters. This is an example of what J. J. Gibson called an affordance (see the 'Affordances' section in Chapter 1, p. 7, for a discussion).

PowerPoint has had bad press in e-learning circles, and it can take a bit of thought to use it to design a really engaging presentation. At its worst, PowerPoint can distort content, reduce student activity and interactivity and lead students to produce business pitches rather than coherent arguments. So, linear presentations can easily (and often do) end up as both unengaging and inefficient as a means of information transfer. Some of the common mistakes are:

- Too many slides – no presentation remains interesting indefinitely!
- Bullet points as the sole or main slide structure
- Content simplified to fit on a slide
- No interactivity or cognitive activation – missed opportunities to stimulate thinking and interaction
- Unnecessary animation – this simply adds to extraneous cognitive load
- Lack of useful animation, e.g. in presenting each part of a complex idea one at a time in order to manage intrinsic cognitive load
- A single route through a sequence of slides – this is desirable when the content should be looked at in a sequence, e.g. when solving an equation, but not necessarily otherwise
- Too much or too little information on a slide – this depends on several factors, most importantly whether the presentation is viewed alone or with a verbal commentary

HOWEVER, PowerPoint and similar alternatives like Google Slides simply allow you to put information on a (small or large) screen. You don't have to fall into any of the aforementioned traps. It's a question of understanding the affordances. While tools like PowerPoint have the potential to display multiple forms of information in multiple ways, they *look like* tools for creating sequences of bullet point-dominated slides. Once you realise this, you can make a conscious decision to use the software differently.

Strategies to cheat death by presentation

Adapt your presentation according to its purpose

The first question to ask yourself when designing a presentation is what it's for. If your presentation is there to stimulate a class discussion or to aid recall of prior learning, then a single slide with an image, statement or question may be all you need.

If it's hard to see who engaged with the image (shown in Figure 2.1) – for example, if the lesson is remote – consider a different technology that allows students to record their response for you to check. You could achieve this using a MS Teams, Moodle Timeline or Google Classroom stream or 'assignment' (the latter should really be called 'task,' as it doesn't need to be used for formal assessments). Or you have multiple options in a full VLE set-up.

If your presentation is to support synchronous delivery of a topic chunk, you will clearly need more than one slide! You still have decisions to make, though, in particular about how much information to put on a slide. A presentation designed to be used to support a live lesson (whether physically present or remote) is a different beast to one designed to be the main source of information:

- If the presentation is to support live delivery – or includes audio narration – you should have relatively little information on a slide. Otherwise, you risk high levels of extraneous cognitive load.
- If the presentation is to be browsed independently and it is the main source of information, you can and probably should put more detail on slides.

Figure 2.1 This picture of a paella could make up a single slide presentation and stimulate questions like 'what is this?' and 'why am I showing you this today?'

Cut down on bullet points

There are times when bullet points work well – for example, when explaining learning outcomes for a lesson or listing the topics to revise for an exam. Most of the time, however, information doesn't fit neatly into bullet points. Presentations dominated by bullet points tend to distort content and make presentations dull to watch. This is made worse when schools and colleges have crude policies, e.g. four bullet points per slide (what happens if the material has three or five elements?).

> **Top tech tip**: If your school or college has or is considering a house style for presentations, *do* standardise colours in order to meet accessibility standards, but think twice about rigid restrictions for number of bullets or font size; the former just distorts content, and both depend on whether the presentation is there to support a taught lesson or as the primary source of information.

So, what to have instead of bullet points? Flow charts, spider diagrams and concept maps can work well, especially if each element can be animated. Video is also good, BUT ensure the embedded video travels with the presentation as it gets passed between colleagues and posted online. An embed from a site like YouTube is often more reliable than an attached video file.

Use animation wisely

Animation can be one of the great strengths of presentation technology, but it is often used badly. Think of this in terms of cognitive load (see the 'Cognitive load theory' section in Chapter 1, p. 7). Animation for its own sake, such as a sentence spinning into view over

14 Presenting content for knowledge transfer

a few seconds or flying around the slide, just creates extraneous cognitive load, i.e. it uses up limited working memory resources without adding any productive information processing. One simple way to improve your presentations is to get rid of extraneous animation.

However, when used appropriately, animation can be used to manage the intrinsic cognitive load of an idea, improving the quality of its processing. Say an idea has three main elements. The total intrinsic cognitive load of those elements may stretch the capacity of working memory. However, using animation, you can view each element separately before putting them together. See Figure 2.2 for an example.

Add interactivity through tasks and menus

Even a well-designed presentation with appropriate animation and a sensible volume of information will lose students' interest sooner or later. You can reduce this by presenting tasks

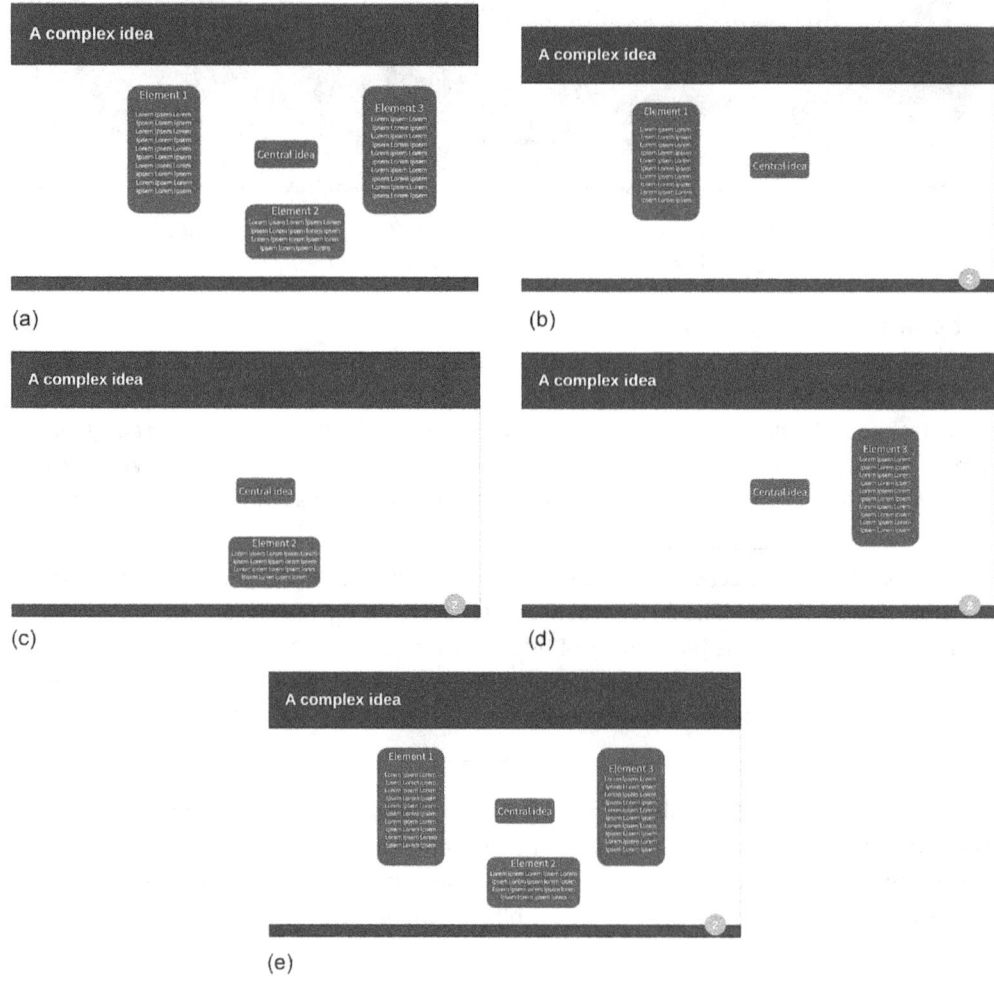

Figure 2.2 (a) Slide with multiple elements; (b) Slide with central and one peripheral element; (c) Slide with central and one peripheral element; (d) Slide with central and one peripheral element; (e) Slide with central and one peripheral element.

Presenting content for knowledge transfer 15

as well as information on slides. Applications like the H5P interactive presentation tool and the presentation tools in Nearpod and Quizizz are designed to facilitate this, but you can add interactivity to any slide. Once again, it's a question of affordances; the aforementioned interactive presentation tools *look like* they are meant to create interactivity, PowerPoint and Google Slides don't. You can still achieve it to some extent, though, with a bit of outside-the-box thinking.

The simplest strategy is to intersperse your content slides with some questions. See Figure 2.3.

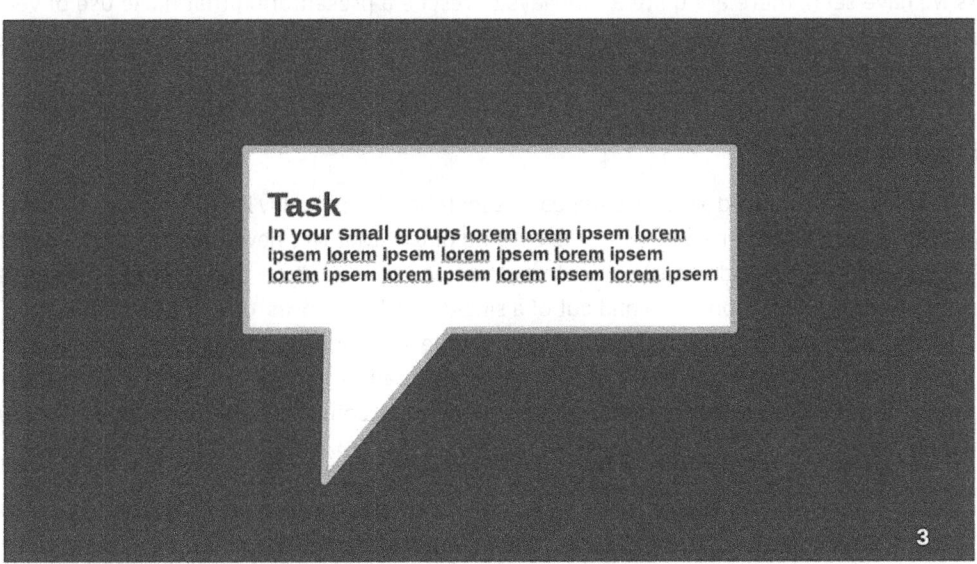

Figure 2.3 Slide with a task instruction.

16 *Presenting content for knowledge transfer*

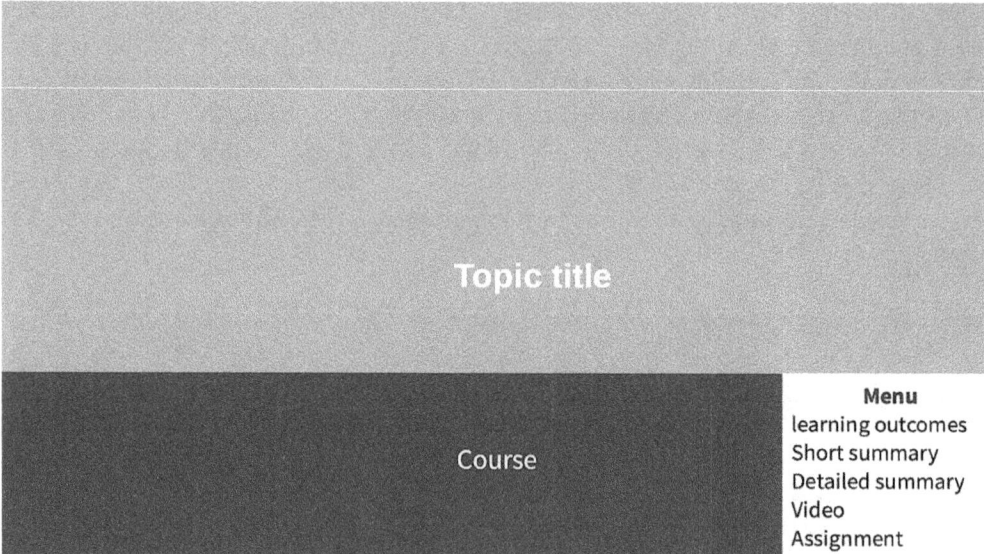

Figure 2.4 A presentation with a menu.

You can also introduce menus so that students don't have to plough through the whole presentation. This may be particularly effective because a degree of cognitive activation is needed to make informed choices from a menu. Put another way, it introduces germane cognitive load (choosing), whilst reducing extraneous cognitive load (reading unwanted material).

Alternatives to traditional presenters

As we have seen, there are quite a few ways to rescue a presentation that make use of very conventional presentation software. However, there are also alternative presentation tools that might suit your needs better.

Zooming presenters

Once you have introduced a menu to a linear presentation, it isn't really linear anymore. However, you can go a step further and use a different kind of tool that was never designed to be linear. Presenters like Prezi and Focuski start from the non-linear position that instead of separate slides you present by zooming in and out of a single 'slide' or 'canvas' of virtually infinite size.

There are risks to this approach – some people experience nausea when slides zoom too violently or in 3D – but it is a great way to escape the linearity of multi-slide presentation tools. I would suggest that zooming presenters come into their own in particular situations:

- When your presentation is used to support a free-flowing class discussion on a new topic, in which you know roughly what ideas you want to cover but not the order in which they will come up. Zooming into an area of resources you have pre-identified as relevant to each subtopic is much more efficient than looking for the right slide.

Presenting content for knowledge transfer 17

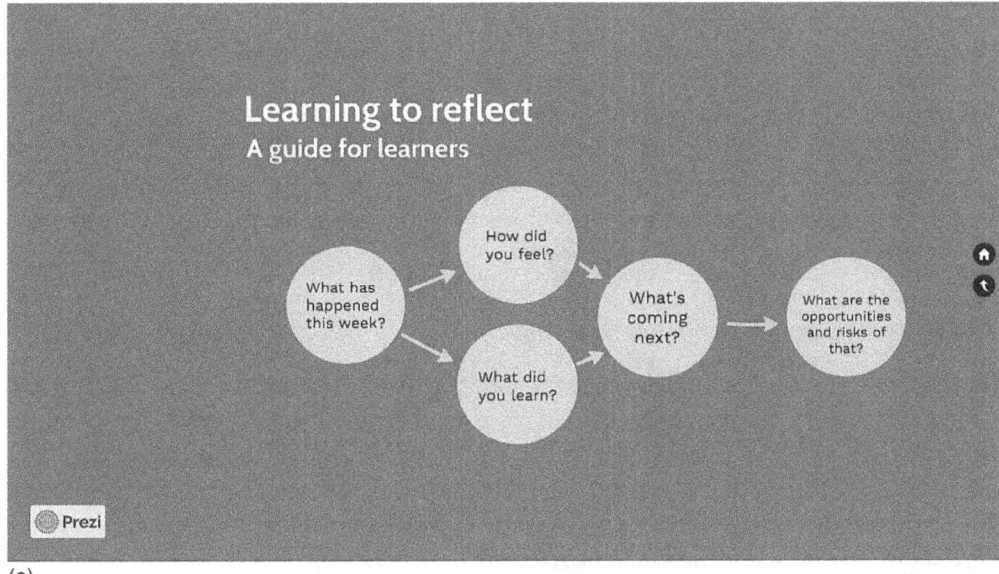

(a)

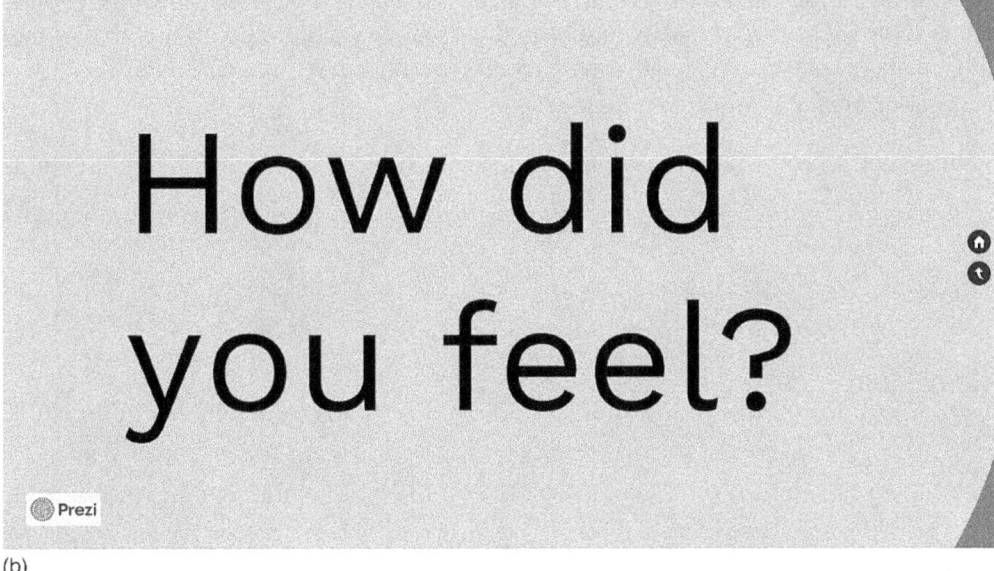

(b)

Figure 2.5 (a) Prezi example of a whole canvas; (b) Prezi example of a zoomed in area.

- When you are reviewing potential assessments and you can zoom in and out of exam papers, mark schemes, student answers and examiners' reports in line with the flow of discussion or particular student questions. As in the first example, you probably can't predict every question and every direction the discussion might take, so it is important to be able to choose the sequence in which you show content in real time – this is a relatively clumsy process in a multi-slide tool.

18 *Presenting content for knowledge transfer*

- During content revision – you can display a textbook or all your handouts or web pages page by page on a zoomable canvas and zoom into each topic as required. It can be helpful when revising to be able to switch at will between visualising the whole and each part.
- When you are trying to stimulate creative thinking. Creative thinking is in some ways the opposite of logical sequential thinking, in which ideas have a single route through them. The latter may indeed be better served by a pre-set sequence of slides, but these may stifle more creative, free-flowing thought.

The H5P Interactive Presentation Tool

If you have access to H5P or Lumi Education, this can be a real game changer – even more so than Prezi was a decade ago. H5P/Lumi shatters the glass ceiling of what a teacher can reasonably be expected to do with technology and puts you firmly in the realm of content normally associated with professional Learning Technologists and Instructional Designers. The most widely used H5P/Lumi tool is the Interactive Presentation Tool. The key difference here is the range of interactive content you can bring to a slide.

The H5P Interactive Presentation Tool takes a little while to get used to because there are no templates – you insert every colour, shape and link manually. However, as well as conventional static content, you have the flexibility to add turning cards, quiz questions, drag-and-drop, mark-the-words, interactive video and downloadable text-input which can serve as a note-taking area or prose-writing exercise.

Figure 2.6 The H5P presentation interface.

Correct answers to quiz questions can be revealed straight away or on a final slide. If you connect your H5P to a VLE or other learning record system (LRS) like that available at H5P. com, marks are automatically stored. This takes flipped and independent learning to a whole new level because you can easily check not only that students engaged with the presentation, but how well they grasped it.

If you don't have institutional access to H5P (it's available as a free Moodle plug-in and a fairly pricey standalone platform), you can create an account at CurrikiStudio (https://currikistudio.org) – this gives you free access to H5P tools like the Interactive Presentation Tool. Presentations are web-based so you can simply add the link to platforms like MS Teams and Google Classroom. Note that CurrikiStudio is hosted in the United States and is not therefore GDPR-compliant. Don't sign your students up or encourage them to create accounts.

The Lumi desktop app allows you to make H5P interactives and save them as HTML5 files as well as H5P and SCORM VLE packages. The HTML5 files can be downloaded from a Google or an Office 365 environment and opened in a browser (Chrome works best; don't even think about Internet Explorer).

> **Top tech tip**: The H5P Interactive Presentation Tool seamlessly brings together delivery and assessment. Try it for flipped learning and get a very good idea which students engaged and how well they understood the material.

Mind map and concept map presenters

Although mind maps and concept maps have different theoretical roots, they look and behave pretty similarly. Both allow you to construct diagrams consisting of connected nodes, which can be text, images or videos. Connectors represent the relationships between node contents. Concept mapping tools tend to offer greater flexibility in structure than classic mind maps. For purposes of this chapter, we are really concerned with flexible mapping tools with attractive templates and a proper presentation mode, meaning you can progress through the nodes in sequence. I discuss mapping tools further in the context of exam preparation in Chapter 3 (p. 44).

Other useful presentation tools

There are any number of presentation tools around, but the majority have very similar features to the standard linear tools. However, for me, a couple of other presenters are particularly worthy of note for specific features. These are either free or have free versions:

- *Emaze*: The distinctive feature of Emaze is its range of templates, including some in 3D. This means for example that art teachers and students can display art in a virtual 3D art gallery. If it isn't directly subject-relevant be wary of 3D – it can create extraneous cognitive load – but it can look great where the relevance is clear.

Table 2.1 Recommended presenters

Recommended for:	Presenter
Generic linear	PowerPoint, Google Slides, Impress
Zooming canvas	Prezi, Focuski
3D templates	Emaze
Embedded websites	Slides.com, Prezi, DeckDeckGo
Presentable diagrams	Miro
Integrated polling	DeckDeckGo
Interactive features	H5P Interactive Presentation Tool

- *Slides.com*: Slides.com is from my perspective one of the best-designed presenters in general, but its killer feature is the ability to embed a webpage within a slide. This means you can demonstrate websites seamlessly in a presentation.
- *DeckDeckGo*: This is distinguished by its embedding abilities, including code of multiple types and a particularly convenient built-in polling tool.

Multimedia

By multimedia I mostly mean audio and video. There are a number of reasons why you should always at least consider multimedia in your plans to make information available to learners:

- It has a neat cultural fit with the way people – especially young people – usually learn in informal contexts.
- It is accessible to students who, for a variety of reasons, struggle with reading prose.
- It provides choice and variety – the agency involved in choosing a medium constitutes germane cognitive load, while the experience of learning through different media helps develop cognitive flexibility – a futureproofing employability skill.

Video streaming

In informal learning situations, learning has become almost synonymous with YouTube. If you want to learn how to change the oil in your car or remove a carpet stain, the chances are that YouTube will be one of your first ports of call. As well as providing a huge number of potentially illuminating videos, YouTube offers free accounts in which you can both curate existing videos and upload your own. Each video or playlist has a link that you can share with students synchronously or asynchronously.

> **Top tech tip**: You can make your YouTube videos public, private or unlisted. Making your work videos public may discomfit your employer because of the difficulty in maintaining intellectual property, but if they are private, it isn't straightforward to share the link. The 'unlisted' option is a good compromise. Videos are hard for unintended audiences to find, but a simple link makes them available to the intended viewers.

Presenting content for knowledge transfer 21

Parts of speech

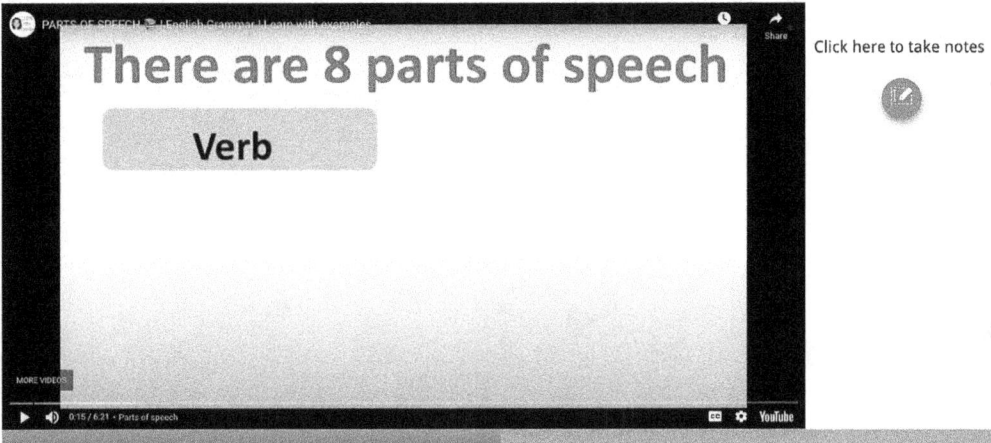

Figure 2.7 H5P slide with embedded video and note taking.

Video teaching hacks

Although video streaming is an essential element of modern teaching, it isn't a panacea, and you still have to plan it. These tips might help:

- Be explicit about what your students are expected to do with a video and, if you are using it in a live lesson, how long it is and what you expect them to do or be able to do after watching it.
- Although you don't want to overload students with video and written information, your video need not occupy a whole screen. If you have a note-taking function as with H5P, you can place this on the same page as a video.
- Keep it short. I'm highly distrustful of the very specific times bandied about supposedly representing student attention span – this will vary according to age, motivation, academic level and probably several other factors. Generally, though, the shorter the better, and if your video is more than five minutes or so consider dividing it into two or more tasks.
- Use start and stop times when sharing long videos. YouTube have released a really useful clipping tool that allows you to share a section of video.
- Consider making the video interactive with a dedicated tool like H5P/Lumi Education Interactive video or by embedding YouTube videos with start and end times in each question in MS or Google Forms. The H5P/Lumi method is a much more comprehensive solution if you have access to the technology, but you can muddle through with office suites technology if you need to.

Screen recording

This is often something that trainers and technologists get much more excited about than teachers or students! However, there are times when you want to record yourself giving a

22 Presenting content for knowledge transfer

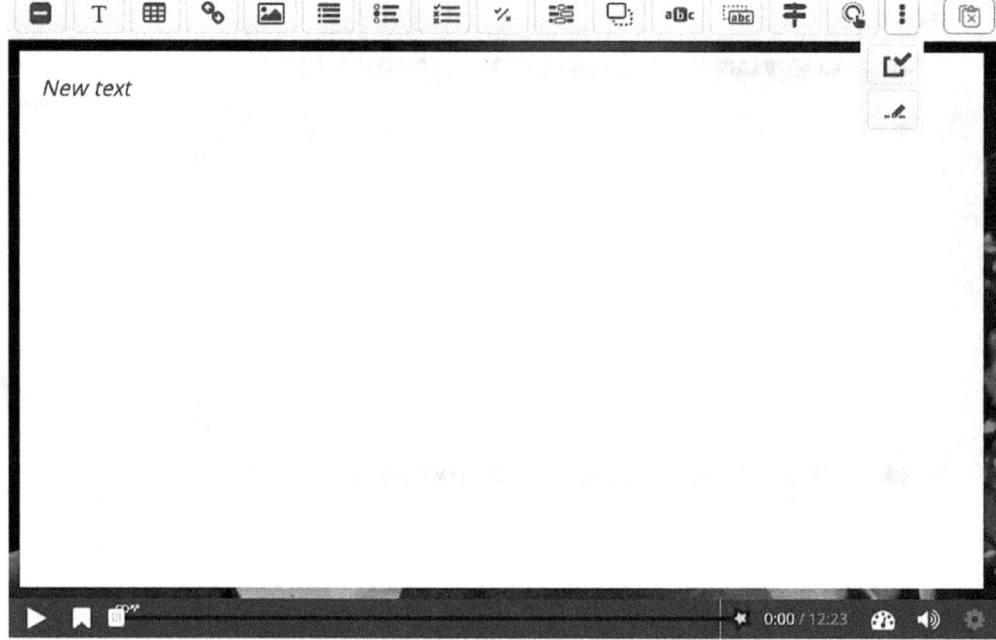

Figure 2.8 The H5P video interface.

presentation, e.g. when you are preparing an asynchronous lesson or showing your students how to access a new site or application. There are various ways to record your screen, and there is the question of narration – including talking head and audio-only options.

Online recording tools
- *Screencastify and Screencast-o-matic* are standard online tools with free versions. These are both available as browser add-ons and provide a very similar user experience. Screencastify is perhaps marginally easier to use but only gives you free recordings up to five minutes, whereas Screencast-o-matic allows 15 minutes.
- *StoryExpress* is a similar idea but is worthy of a separate entry because it has a generous free version with some really nice features, including the ability to start with full-screen face and then reduce face size once you are showing the screen.

Desktop applications
- *Camtasia* is the industry standard. It is powerful and user-friendly, but pricey.
- *Open Broadcast Studio* is an advanced free and open-source alternative. It is probably the most versatile and powerful option but requires a slightly steeper learning curve than the alternatives.

Screen-recording hacks
- *Music*: If the purpose of your video is to inspire – for example, you are demonstrating a range of features on a website, an upbeat musical background might be a good thing. If the purpose is to put across important information – e.g. a subject-related presentation – then music probably just provides extraneous cognitive load and should be avoided.

- *Video narration*: Most modern screen-recorders allow you to speak over your recorded screen. If you are hoping to simulate a live lesson but are delivering asynchronously, then this is clearly the most lifelike option. However, it is advisable to provide an audio-over-screencast option to reduce visual distraction and extraneous cognitive load in the visual channel.
- *Host it on YouTube*: With a free YouTube account, you can ensure that viewers have access to captions, a transcript and the ability to vary video speed. Because of the high cognitive load in narrated videos, these accessibility features can be really useful.
- *As with any video, keep it short*: A short sequence of stimulus material followed by engaging activity is generally the way to go when it comes to securing student engagement.
- *It can still be interactive*: Screencasts benefit as well as any instructional video from questions, choices and note-taking exercises.

Working with audio

You might ask in these days of interactive video and immersive environments whether there is still a place for simple audio. Spoiler alert – the correct answer is yes! One reason for this is accessibility. This is not a nod to the thoroughly debunked idea of learning styles, but there is no doubt that some students, including many with dyslexia, low literacy and low visual acuity, process verbal information better through an auditory channel than via a visual channel. Less obvious but equally important, some students with visual and working memory problems will make better use of audio than video.

A second reason to consider audio also relates to equality of opportunity but in a quite different sense. You may have students who are short on the time required to give undivided and sustained visual attention to video or text. In some cases, these students can make good use of audio because they are able to listen while doing other things. They might, for example, have a long bus journey to and from school or college, or they might have a solitary, cognitively undemanding job. In both these scenarios the auditory channels in students' working memory will be underutilised, and there is available capacity for processing auditory information.

Obtaining audio versions of resources

It is relatively straightforward to obtain audio versions of other files:

- *Text-to-audio*: Numerous speech-generator sites allow you to paste text or upload a Word file and choose a voice to read it out. Generally, these sites have a limit on how much text you can convert free of charge per day, and they offer a premium service. Which site provides best value will probably vary over time but I am currently using ttsMP3.com (https://ttsmp3.com/).

> **Top tech tip**: Most text-to-speech sites offer a similar range of standard voices, and I find that they vary considerably in quality. I strongly recommend Amy (British English) and Geraint (Welsh English) for female and male voices respectively.

24 *Presenting content for knowledge transfer*

- *Video-to-audio*: If you have a video file like an mp4, you can either create an audio version using a desktop application like VLC or QuickTime Player or by means of a web service like FreeConvert.com. If you want an audio version of a YouTube video, there are a range of sites which allow you to enter a YouTube video URL and download a corresponding audio file. I currently like WTMP3 (https://ytmp3.cc/youtube-to-mp3/), but if this doesn't work well for you, there are plenty of alternatives.
- *Zoom-to-audio*: All online meeting/remote teaching applications allow you to download a video file of recorded meetings. Zoom has the useful additional feature of allowing you to download an audio file as well. Make sure you use the record online option.

Audio hacks

- Students will probably access audio files on mobile devices. Make sure that, however you send them or make them available to students, the files can be accessed from a mobile device.
- Audio files are small compared to video files, but all the same, if you can give them to students while they are on a school/college Wi-Fi, that will save them from using mobile data that some won't be able to spare. Similarly, make sure that audio files are downloadable, as opposed to just playing online.
- Someone WILL ask you if it's true that listening to audio in their sleep (or while drifting off to sleep) helps them learn stuff. The answer is, sadly, a big no. It's an extremely pervasive myth, so I would at least be prepared for it and consider bringing it up.
- Audio files probably won't contain much information about what topic they are intended for or what mental schemas the information therein is intended for. This makes sense – no

Figure 2.9 An audio file with questions on an H5P Interactive Presentation slide.

Presenting content for knowledge transfer 25

one wants to listen to a real-time voice talking through units and topics at the start of an audio file. It means, however, that you need to make sure that, wherever or however you make the files available, they are accompanied by this kind of meta-level information. This might be in the file title or a file description.
- Think carefully about whether audio resources need to be accompanied by activities or assessment. If you are envisioning them being listened to while a student is working or en route to or from you, then perhaps not. However, if your reason for using audio is more because of the way the student likes to process information, then anything that encourages engagement and cognitive activation is well worth considering. You could, for example, drop an audio file into a single-slide H5P interactive presentation and place a question with it.

Podcasting

You may, of course, never need to record your own audio if your use of sound is based on providing audio alternatives to other resource formats for accessibility reasons. You may, however, wish to podcast. Podcasting is often not well understood; real podcasting has three elements:

1. Audio files of monologue or discussions are recorded and made available online to students or other consumers.
2. More than one issue is published. Usually, though not always, podcasts are regular events.
3. Students are notified automatically when a new issue of the podcast is published.

Podcasts can be used to supplement or consolidate lessons, to accompany and clarify homework or flipped tasks, or they might be one of your approaches to supporting a revision programme.

If you have a Moodle VLE, the easiest way to podcast is using the PCast plugin. PCast gives you the option of vodcasting (video podcasts as opposed to audio); whether this is an advantage depends – as discussed earlier. Otherwise, I would use the excellent and free Anchor Service (https://anchor.fm). Unlike other free podcasting services Anchor handles the whole podcasting process from recording to publishing in an extremely well-designed and user-friendly interface.

E-books

In these days of live remote teaching and interactive online resources, you might well ask whether there is still a place for the humble e-book. I would answer that in two ways. First, yes there is. Although dense text does not work well on a computer or even a tablet screen, e-readers like the Kindle and Kobo are well designed to simulate the experience of reading words on a paper page. They allow comfortable reading of a conventional book in digital form.

Being able to access extensive text on a handheld device opens up a host of study environments outside the classroom. So, a student can read up ahead of a lesson or as the beginning of a revision programme in a garden, on a train or a beach. Whilst many young people eschew

26 *Presenting content for knowledge transfer*

dense text and prefer multimedia environments, the other side of the coin is that reading extended prose is a transferable skill that most tech solutions fail to develop.

Second, an e-book doesn't have to be that humble. I personally like text-only e-books, provided I'm reading them on a suitable device, but a modern e-book can incorporate multimedia and interactivity.

Making a conventional e-book

It is surprisingly easy to make a decent e-book. The industry-standard tool for doing this is *Calibre* (shown in Figure 2.10). Calibre is free and open source and works on all major desktop operating systems. The full programme doesn't work on mobile platforms, but there are Android and iOS apps that allow you to access, share and read files from your desktop device.

Calibre takes existing files, such as Word documents and PDFs, and converts them into the e-book format of your choice. Your choice of format depends on the device on which your students will read the book. Kindles work best with .mobi, .azw and .azw3 files. Other devices use .epub. So, if you make two versions available, .mobi and .epub, you should cover virtually all the bases. To edit an e-book save it in .epub format and open with Sigil.

Multimedia interactive e-books

The multimedia interactive book (MIB) is a different beast altogether and is designed for different devices and situations. In fact, it's only nominally a book, and each 'page' can be text, video, audio, an embedded web page or a quiz or other interactivity (or more than one of these in a column). Because you will almost certainly be using this kind of book on a conventional screen as opposed to an e-reader, it is a really good idea to keep text to a minimum and make use of the available multimedia.

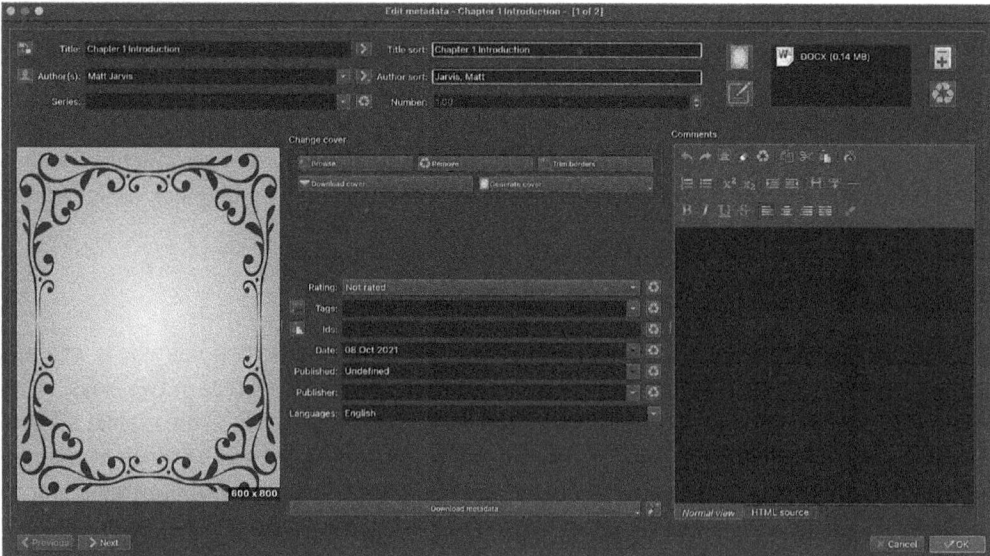

Figure 2.10 The Calibre interface.

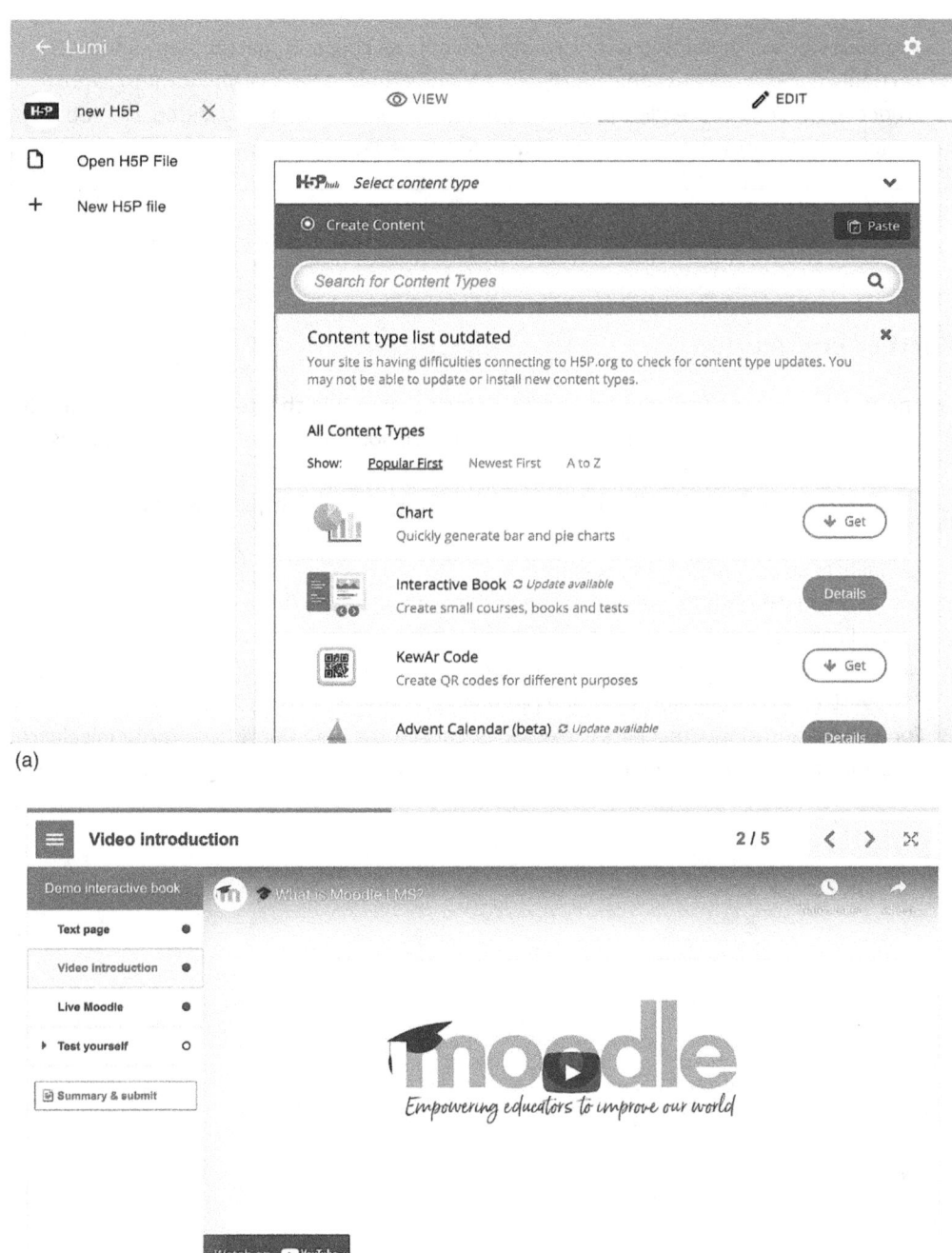

Figure 2.11 (a) Creating an MIB in Lumi; (b) a video page in an MIB.

> **Top tech tip**: You might well want to make use of both conventional text-only and MIBs. Text-only books work best on an e-reader and for situations where you want to expose students to dense, extended prose. Multimedia books work on a desktop or mobile device and can provide a complete flipped or blended learning experience.

You can make an MIB using H5P or Lumi. An example is shown in Figure 2.11.

Further information

There may well be a few applications I've referred to in this chapter that you may not be familiar with, so here are some links to follow up some of the most important ones:
Prezi: https://prezi.com
H5P (interactive presentations, video, audio and e-books): https://h5p.com
Lumi: https://app.lumi.education
Calibre: https://calibre-ebook.com

For a set of H5P/Lumi training resources, try this: https://h5p.org/content-types-and-applications

Here is an interesting discussion on the role of audio in teaching and learning: https://reverb.chat/blog/audio-restoring-communication-students-teachers/

For a discussion of why teachers use e-books, consult the following: https://britannicalearn.com/blog/top-10-reasons-teachers-are-using-e-books/

3 Digital assessment

By the end of this chapter, you should be able to:

- Know a range of tools and strategies to assess and respond to learner progress
- Distinguish between baseline, formative and summative assessment and target appropriate tools to each
- Appreciate valid and pedagogically led digital assessment decisions including the importance of low-stakes assessment
- Understand what is meant by adaptivity and introduce adaptivity to formative assessment
- Understand what is meant by reflective learning and introduce a range of reflective tools to your assessment practice
- Introduce gamification to formative assessment
- Use technology, including mapping tools, adaptive flashcards and prose-planning tools, to help students prepare for exams

This chapter is concerned with using technology to assess student progress. Clearly, most assessment takes place not in a vacuum (exams being the exception) but as part of lessons, live or remote, or as an independent learning activity preceding or following a lesson. Assessment therefore warrants the same considerations as other aspects of teaching and learning. It needs to be clear and accessible, appropriately located in the context of other activities and, most importantly, serve a clear purpose. We should see assessment not as a bolt-on, but as central to teaching. This chapter is also intended to help you make sense of some of the current buzzwords in digital education. I explore examples of adaptive learning, reflective learning and gamification.

A quick recap on assessment

Before we consider digital assessment, let's take a moment to recall what assessment actually is. There are three broad purposes for assessing students:

- *Baseline assessment*: Baseline or initial assessment takes place when we first meet a student or when they start a new Key Stage. It provides us with an initial level against which to track individual progress and can be used as a basis for setting goals and putting students on different learning pathways.

- *Formative assessment*: Formative assessment or assessment for learning (not to be confused with *Assessment for Learning*, a much narrower model of assessment) takes place during learning with the aim of optimising the learning.
- *Summative assessment*: This is intended to measure an individual's level after learning has taken place. The classic examples are GCSEs and A-levels; however, summative assessment need not take place after a programme of learning is completed, just at the point where a particular body of learning can be assumed to be ready to assess. Unit tests and portfolio assignments are examples of summative assessments that take place during a course.

Baseline assessment

Baseline assessment can involve measures ranging from informal observation to standardised tests. We might assess students at the start of a learning programme for a range of variables:

- Numeracy
- Literacy
- IT skills
- Subject-specific knowledge
- Indicators of dyslexia and Scotopic Stress Syndrome (visual stress)
- Education readiness – holistic measures that might include communication, self-care and attitudes to learning

Commercial packages

You can buy off-the-shelf paper packs of baseline assessments tailored to your age group and subject; however, it is far more convenient to assess online so that marking is done for you and results can be readily accessed. A number of commercial online platforms, e.g. BKSB (www.bksb.co.uk) and ForSkills (www.ncfe.org.uk/skills-assessment/), include baseline assessments for numeracy, literacy and employability. These carry a significant cost but are not limited to baseline assessment, offering an impressive range of interactive learning materials.

Creating your own baseline assessment

If you teach something other than maths or English and you want to carry out a baseline assessment, there are some technical options available to you. Google and Microsoft Forms are both well suited for this task. The essentials are that you need to be able to create multiple-choice questions or grids (called Likert scales in MS Forms), and that you have the option to view responses after submission. There is no compulsion to baseline-assess, so if you do so, it should be for a pedagogically sound reason.

Consider the example in Figure 3.1. Simply assessing the basic skills that might affect how well a new student might take to a new subject like psychology achieves very little in itself, and if you don't have a plan, you're better off not doing it. However, there are a couple of things you can do with this information.

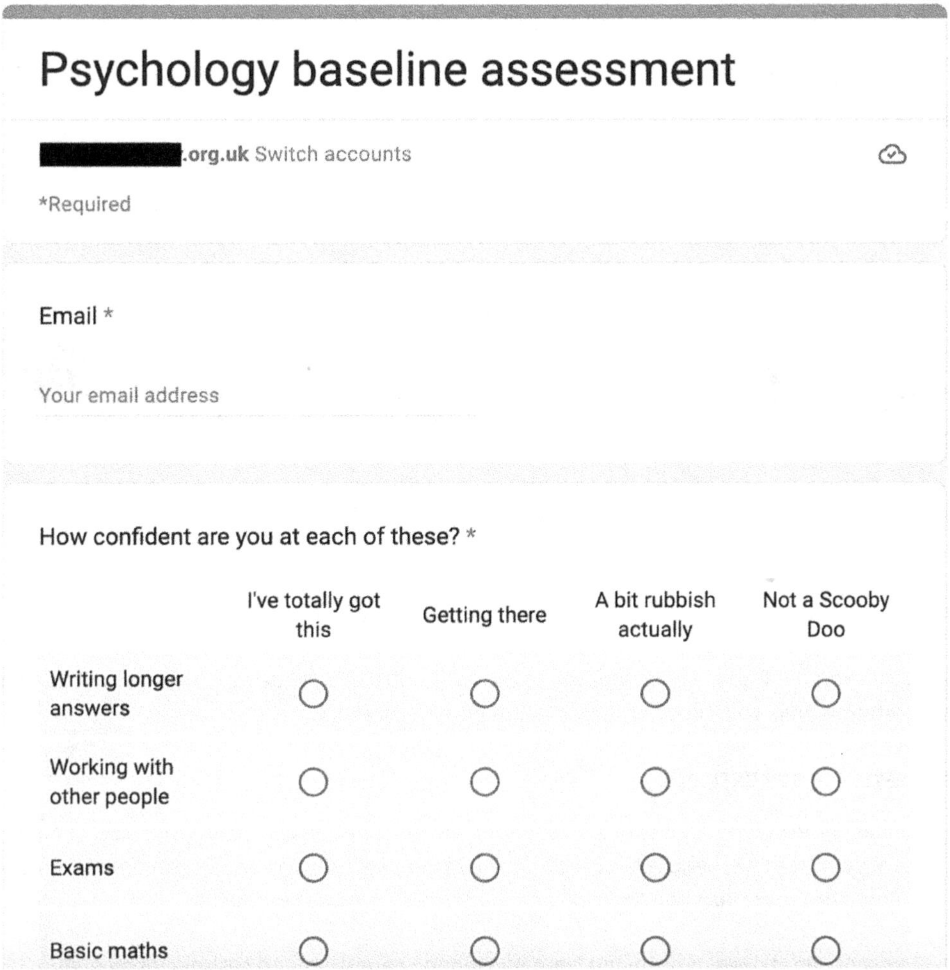

Psychology baseline assessment

▇▇▇▇▇▇▇.org.uk Switch accounts

*Required

Email *

Your email address

How confident are you at each of these? *

	I've totally got this	Getting there	A bit rubbish actually	Not a Scooby Doo
Writing longer answers	○	○	○	○
Working with other people	○	○	○	○
Exams	○	○	○	○
Basic maths	○	○	○	○

Figure 3.1 A Google™ form for baseline assessment.

- Track progress on these skills by repeating the assessment in tutorials, and use the visible progress to boost students' self-efficacy and confidence. The technology is straightforward; just make sure the form settings allow viewing of results and resubmission.
- Make the form adaptive and link low ratings to booster activities. This requires use of the branching questions featured on Forms applications. Branching questions work only with certain question types, so bear this in mind when you design your form.

> **Top tech tip**: We have touched on the idea of adaptivity a couple of times, and as it is central to current teaching practice, let's make sure you are clear on its meaning. To adapt means to change your delivery in real time in response to learner feedback or progress. This can be seen either as a modern version of differentiation or a replacement for it – the idea of labelling students with an ability level and targeting different resources and activities is now widely seen as crude and dated.

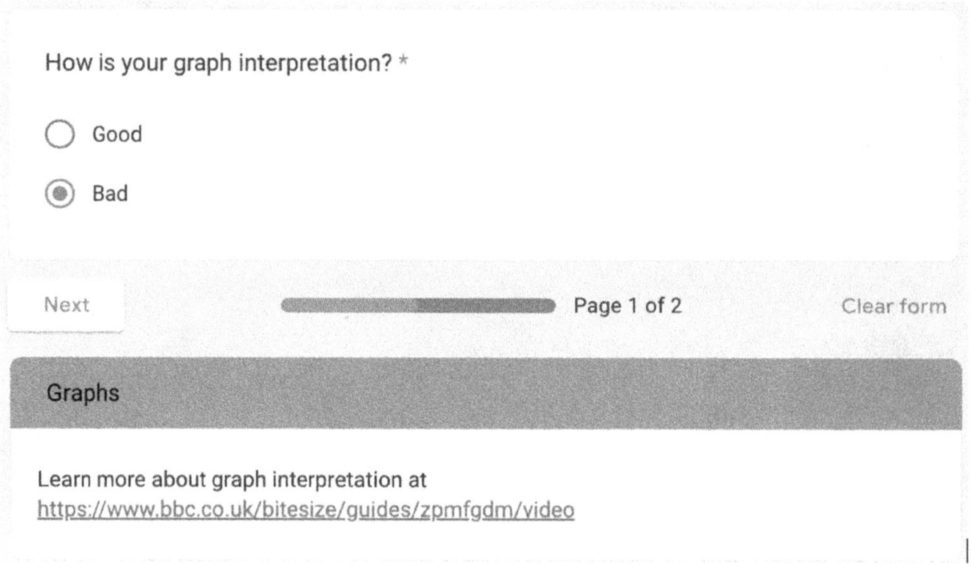

Figure 3.2 A Google™ form used to identify a weakness and link to a booster activity.

In this example (Figure 3.2), a baseline assessment that identifies a weakness with graph interpretation links to a graph-interpretation booster activity.

Formative assessment

If baseline assessment is for most teachers an optional extra, formative assessment is absolutely central to all education, and here learning technology really comes into its own. Remember that there are two key reasons for formative assessment:

1. To practice retrieval, improving both knowledge retention and test performance.
2. To help students and teachers understand what groups and individuals know well and less well.

Technology can help with both of these; online quizzes can check, mark and track student understanding, while presenting revision activities at optimal intervals, adapting to individual student progress. Once set up properly, this kind of technology can radically reduce teacher workload, although some up-front investment of time is required. If you can integrate formative assessment into your knowledge transfer technology well enough, the potential is there to re-imagine the role of the teacher, significantly reducing presentation and marking time, and allowing you to focus on what technology is unlikely to ever do – provide bespoke support for individual student needs.

Retrieval practice and the testing effect

One of the simplest and best-validated ways to improve retention of knowledge is retrieval practice through testing. You probably need a range of testing strategies, including mocks corresponding to the kind of final assessment your students will be subject to. However, mocks are anxiety-provoking and disruptive to day-to-day teaching and learning, and you should provide some kind of non-threatening retrieval practice on a much more regular basis.

Low-stakes formative assessment

Arguably, the key to understanding effective testing is the idea of 'low-stakes assessment.' A formal definition of low-stakes assessment is assessment that does not count towards final grades, but I would argue that actually the key element of low-stakes assessment is that it does not cause anxiety. From a cognitive load perspective, anxiety involves worry which is extraneous cognitive load and reduces short-term memory capacity. The more we can make quizzes a fun process as opposed to a frightening one, the more positive will be not only the quality of student experience but also the impact on performance. To minimise anxiety and be truly low-stakes, formative assessment should probably not link directly to 'working at' grades, and in fact students should probably not be aware of when assessments are recorded at all.

Other factors affecting effectiveness of formative assessment

Low-stakes assessment is important because it takes anxiety away from assessment. You probably also need to consider other aspects of the assessment.

1. *Question difficulty*: Questions need to be hard enough to activate a good level of cognitive processing, but not so hard as to be discouraging.
2. *Time spent on assessment*: Common sense tells us that time spent assessing takes time away from delivery. However, research into the test-potentiation effect has shown that learning increases following an assessment, so you would have to go *really* over the top with time spent assessing before it started to have a negative impact on learning. Generally, I would start, intersperse and finish every lesson with low-stakes assessment of appropriate difficulty.
3. *Humour*: This is a difficult one; research tells us that humour tends to constitute extraneous cognitive load and reduce the efficiency of both delivery and assessment. That's the science. BUT teaching will always be art as well as science, and the art in this case may mean balancing efficiency of knowledge transfer against the benefits of motivating students through engagement and relationship-building. If judicious use of humour means that your students enjoy and engage with you and your lessons, you may find it is still very worthwhile even if some of your quizzes have slightly less impact.
4. *Question type*: I will return to this in more detail in considering the capabilities of different quiz platforms. Briefly, though, I would use a range of question types and use them in ways that make the assessment meaningful and appropriately challenging. There is nothing wrong with multiple-choice questions – the most-used question type – but there are others to consider. Use true-or-false questions sparingly; some research has suggested that these are less effective in enhancing learning than multiple-choice questions.

Formative assessment and tracking

The second major purpose of formative assessment is progress tracking. Whatever platform or platforms you use to assess your students, each will need to automatically keep a record of assessment results. If you use a central digital mark book you will also need an efficient way to transfer results from one to the other. There is nothing wrong incidentally with using your 'base system' – Google Workspace, MS Office or VLE platform – as the site for your digital mark book.

There is more to student tracking than quizzes, however. Self-assessments, goal setting and diarising all lend themselves to the use of learning technology and, well used, can enhance learning.

Self-assessments

The humble checklist can be a straightforward and visual way to ensure both teacher and student know what they have completed and what needs to be done. This applies equally to revising for exams and portfolio completion. Perhaps a better way to self-assess is using multiple-choice questions that break down a course and allow four or five options of self-assessment against each course element. See Figure 3.3 for an example.

The example in Figure 3.3 was created in Moodle, but you can do the same thing with any form creation tool, including MS Office and Google Workspace, provided it allows you the option of viewing previous submissions. This is important, as it means that student and teacher can view submissions separately and together.

ADAPTIVITY

Self-assessment can be adaptive. This is easiest to set up using soft adaptivity rather than hard adaptivity. 'Hard adaptivity' means that choice is taken away from the student and that their score on a test or answer to a question leads them on to a particular predetermined pathway. The alternative is 'soft adaptivity,' in which you suggest different activities according to earlier responses. Figure 3.4 shows a simple example of soft adaptivity in self-assessment of algebraic skills. If the student says they are finding the topic tricky, they are referred to an easier learning resource.

Goal setting

Form technology can also allow you to set learning goals (or targets) with your students. Goal setting as a model of reflective learning (i.e. improving learning through reflection) was very popular a decade ago and has somewhat fallen into disrepute now. This is probably an understandable reaction to the omnipresence of goal setting and the demand to formularise it, making the 'smartness' of goals and the regularity of goal setting the criteria for judgement rather than the relevance and usefulness of the goals. However, done properly, goal setting can be a powerful tool and, like self-assessment, just requires a decent form builder in a system where both teacher and student can revisit, check goals and amend progress against them. An example is shown in Figure 3.5.

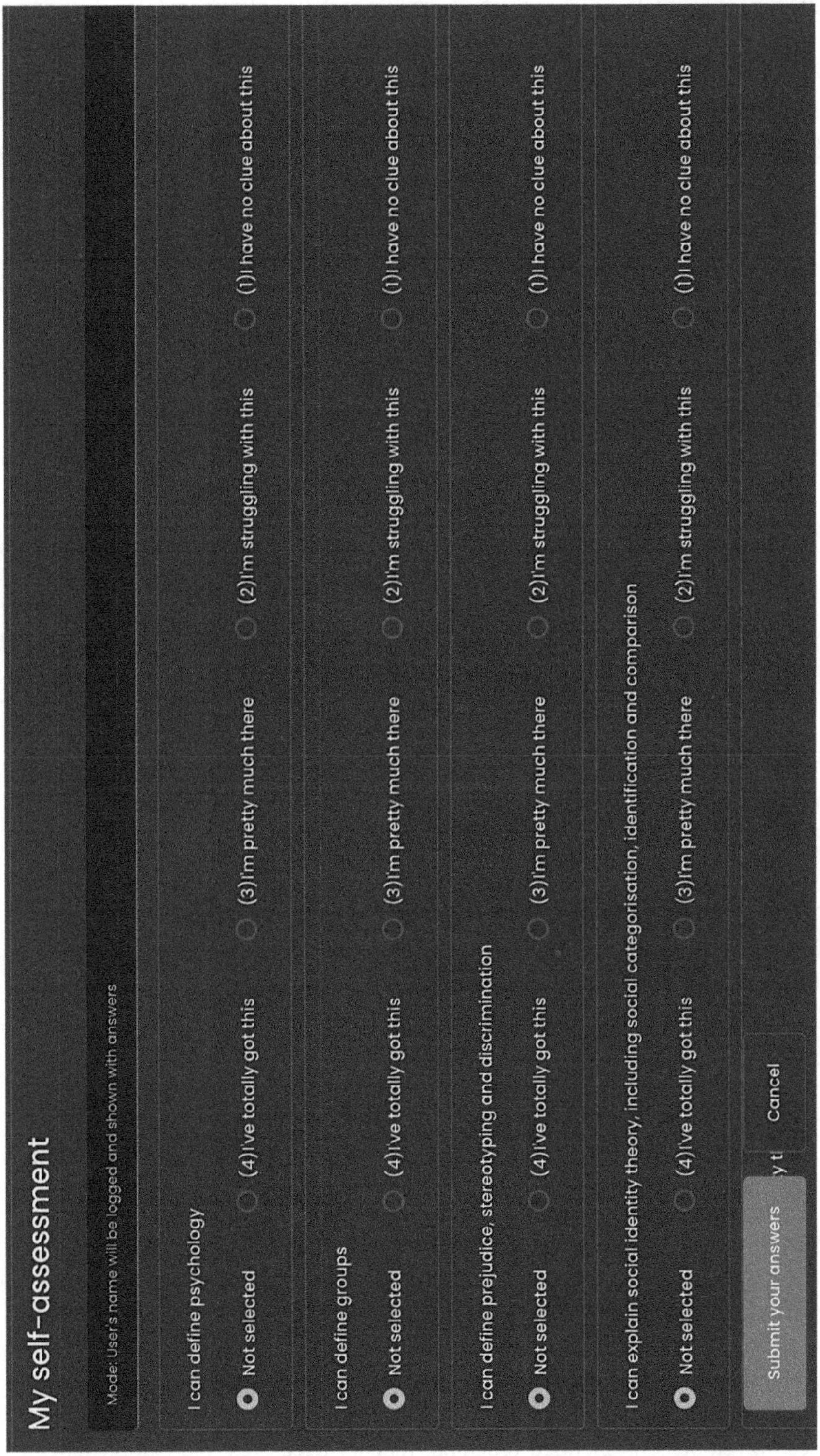

Figure 3.3 A Moodle™ feedback used as a self-assessment tool.

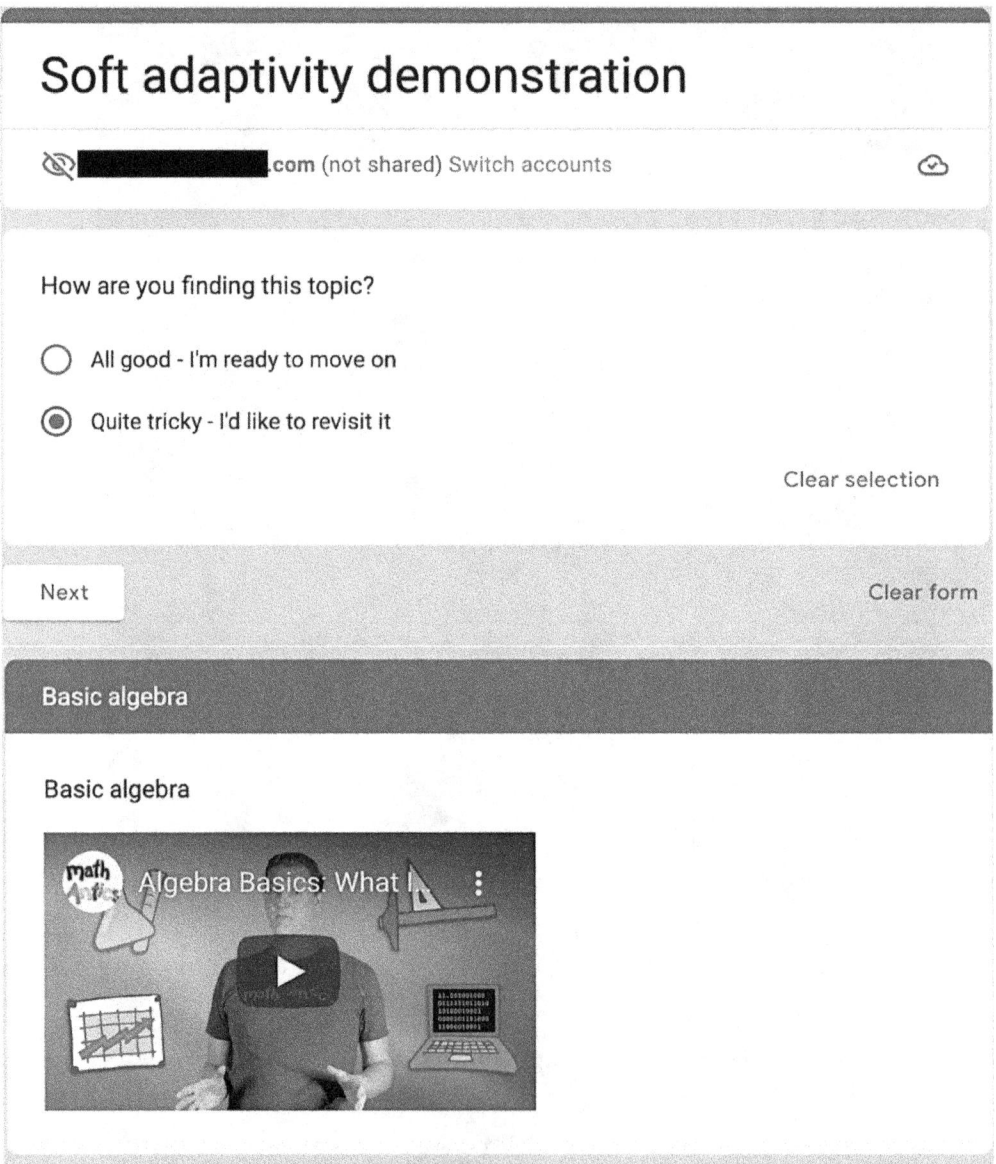

Figure 3.4 A Google™ form where the answer 'Quite tricky' directs the user to a booster video.

Diarisation
Another approach to reflective learning is diarising. This really just means keeping a record – like a diary. The best diarisation tools are those incorporated into Virtual Learning Environment technology – these allow recording in written, audio and video formats and alert teachers to student submissions. Diarisation is particularly useful for vocational courses where reflection forms part of portfolio evidence, and for recording progress in placements and other critical experiences. In remote and blended teaching, teacher-accessible diarisation tools serve a

Figure 3.5 A Moodle™ Feedback used as a goal-setting page.

valuable safeguarding role, as students can check in and teachers can get clues about their mental health from their entries.

Quiz tools

The simplest way to put together a quiz is to use the quiz option on Microsoft or Google Forms. Both these platforms are quite limited in the kinds of quizzes they support, but they do have the advantage of easily and automatically recording results in a mark book teachers can monitor. Remember that, in order to comply with GDPR, you should not upload your student details to external quiz sites, although you can set up a quiz for self-registration as long as students are all at least 13 (the UK age of data consent) and don't use identifiable personal data like real name or email. You may be lucky enough to have an institutional account, but these tend to be quite expensive and your Management may not be easily convinced of the benefits.

Kahoot

Kahoot is arguably the ultimate tool for synchronous (real-time) formative assessment. It is highly gamified (see the 'Gamification' section in this chapter, p. 42, for a discussion) and, for a while at least, tends to be well liked by students, although this can change if teachers overuse it. Kahoot makes it equally easy to create your own quizzes or search for pre-existing ones, which you copy and tweak, potentially saving a huge amount of time.

Although there are premium options, the lifeblood of Kahoot is simple but brilliantly designed multiple-choice questions. Teachers share a link, and students follow it to compete as individuals or teams. They can sign in without using real names, bypassing GDPR issues, but you will need a way to match their account names with real names if you want to be able to track results. Although Kahoot works on any device, it is usually run by a teacher using a desktop device while students respond using mobile devices – an example is shown in Figure 3.6.

H5P

H5P is a suite of interactive tools, including a range of quiz question types. H5P offers a very comprehensive range of question types including the usual true-or-false, multiple choice and short answers but also drag-and-drop (text and images), mark the words and even an 'essay' tool that can self-mark prose by means of key words. If you have a VLE like Moodle, H5P is now built in, and scores are kept in the course grade book. If you don't have a VLE, you can still create H5P quizzes through a free desktop application called Lumi Education and share them as HTML (web page) files, but for full functionality you need a way to record results. At the time of writing, H5P is my personal favourite quiz tool, but only if you have VLE access (Figure 3.7).

One of the most impressive H5P tools, not a quiz as such but certainly a quiz-like formative assessment tool, is the Summary Builder. This is essentially an interactive take on traditional bulleted lists as chapter summaries. It allows students to build their own summary of a topic by answering multiple-choice questions. Each correct answer is added to the summary. An example is shown in Figure 3.8.

Digital assessment   39

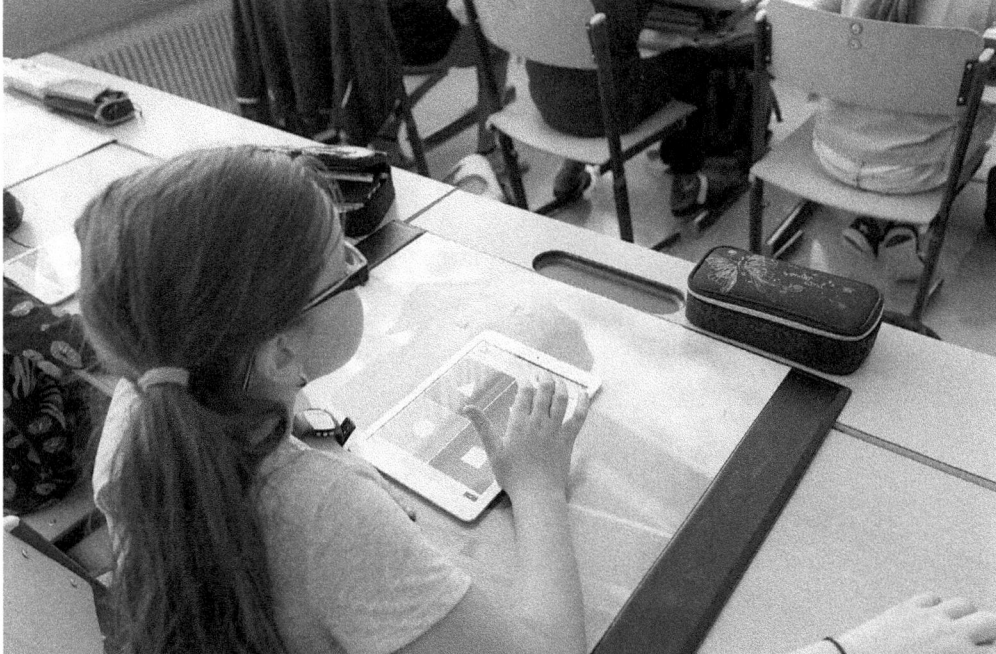

Figure 3.6 Joining a Kahoot quiz on a tablet.

Source: Shutterstock 1879026835

> **Top tech tip**: You can share H5Ps using MS Teams or Google Classroom, but these applications won't directly open the file; you must download the HTML file and open it with a browser from your downloads.

Alternatives

This section will no doubt date quickly as existing applications are improved and new ones come along. Socrative occupies a similar place in the quiz ecosystem; it has the advantage of supporting multiple-choice, true-or-false and short-answer questions. Like Kahoot, Socrative does not require any student data, just sharing a quiz entry code. I don't find the interface as intuitive as Kahoot, but this is just a matter of taste. Quizizz is another tool with a better range of question types and the ability to incorporate these into a very attractive multimedia presentation.

Assignment tools

Assignment tools allow you to set tasks in which students submit answers, perhaps by completing on-screen boxes but more often by uploading documents. If I could rename one thing in the world of digital education, it would be 'assignment' tools. The term 'assignment' refers, especially in vocational education, to a summative assessment. However, I would argue that

40 Digital assessment

At an interview I should always

☐ Ask sensible questions

☐ Assault the interviewer

☐ Try to be as polite as possible

☐ Look smart

☐ Demand to know whether I have the job before leaving

● Check

Figure 3.7 An H5p quiz.

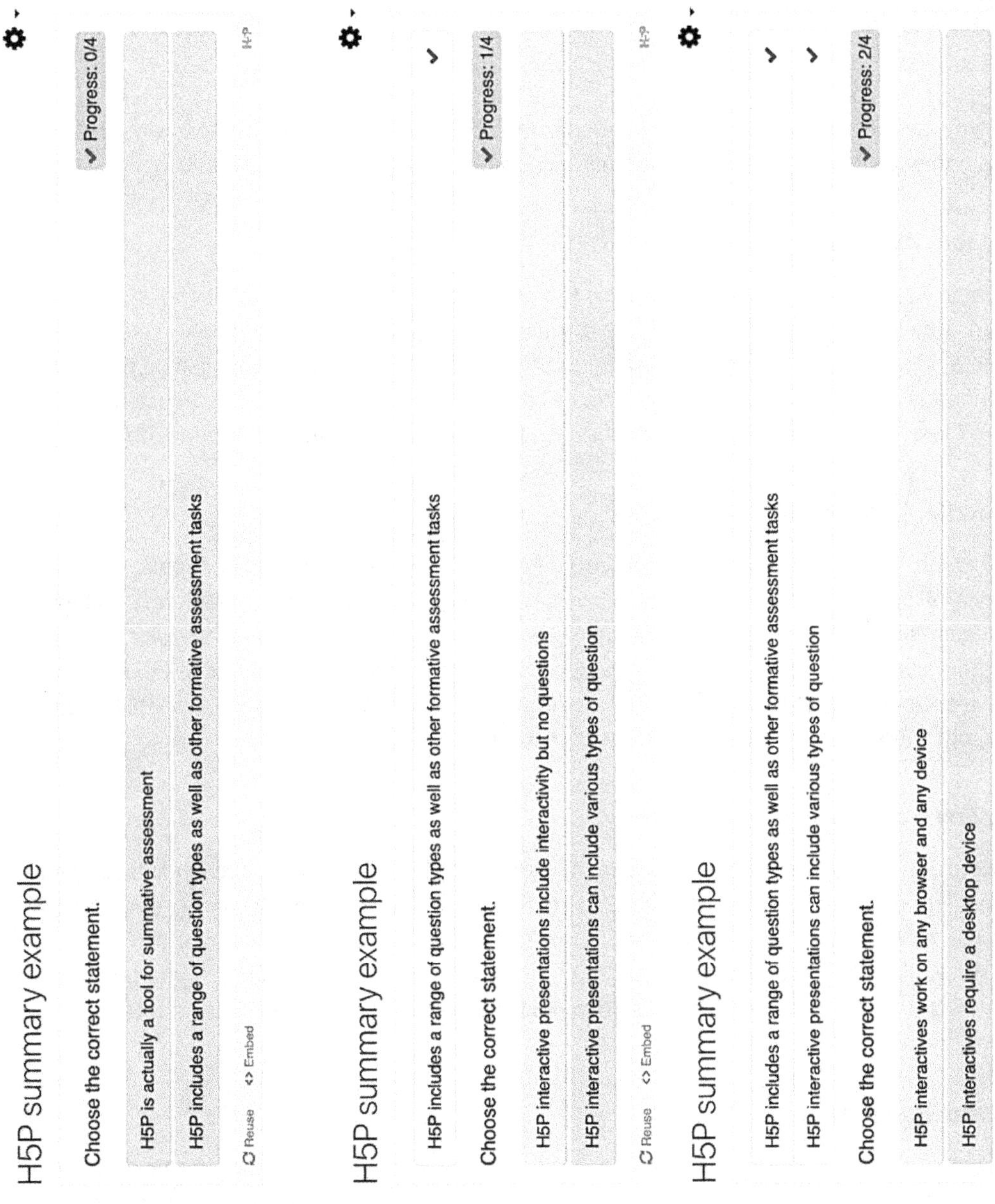

Digital assessment 41

H5P summary example

Choose the correct statement.

- H5P is actually a tool for summative assessment
- H5P includes a range of question types as well as other formative assessment tasks

Progress: 0/4

↻ Reuse <> Embed

H5P summary example

- H5P includes a range of question types as well as other formative assessment tasks

Choose the correct statement.

- H5P interactive presentations include interactivity but no questions
- H5P interactive presentations can include various types of question

Progress: 1/4

↻ Reuse <> Embed

H5P summary example

- H5P includes a range of question types as well as other formative assessment tasks
- H5P interactive presentations can include various types of question

Choose the correct statement.

- H5P interactives work on any browser and any device
- H5P interactives require a desktop device

Progress: 2/4

Figure 3.8 An H5P summary.

assignment tools are actually most useful in the context of formative assessment and should really be called 'tasks.'

> **Top tech tip:** Don't be afraid to use the assignment tools for small homework, classwork, flipped learning tasks and remote tasks. Use it any time you want to check written work from your students, not just for bigger or more formal assignments.

You can potentially use any form builder with a file submission option as a way to collect assignments. To add value to this basic functionality, the following are often used.

Google Assignments

Google Assignments are widely seen as the most user-friendly assignment tool. They come with a built-in plagiarism checker and a range of pre-set phrases for commentary. With a free plug-in you can record voice feedback. Although Google Assignments can be used independently of Google Classroom, they really come into their own when you can use the excellent Classroom comms tools to communicate task details and give formative feedback.

Moodle Assignments

Although Virtual Learning Environments like Moodle have fallen out of favour since the Covid-19 pandemic, they still easily provide the most versatile assignment tools. Moodle Assignments have a tremendous range of configuration options, allowing a choice of standard file submission or writing or recording audio and/or video in an editable box. You also have options for multiple markers and moderation. Plagiarism checkers are available as plug-ins, but there is generally a substantial cost to this.

Online worksheet tools

If you like your assignments in the form of worksheets, it is quite possible to set and complete these online. If you use MS Office or Google Classroom, you can simply share a document to be copied and individually edited. If you use Moodle, you have additional options to complete PDFs within the VLE (e.g. with Amanote plug-ins) and submit for marking. If you don't have a VLE but prefer to work with PDFs you could use something like Live Worksheets (https://liveworksheets.com).

Gamification

I have already touched on gamification in discussing Kahoot. Gamification can be defined as introducing the elements of gaming to digital learning tasks. In practice this can mean quite a range of changes:

- Game-like background music – Kahoot being the obvious example
- Countdown timers limiting the time to complete a task

- Competitive quizzes completed in real time
- Activity feedback involving emojis, animations, sounds, etc.
- Leader boards; individual, team, temporary or enduring in a course
- Badging achievements
- Dedicated games as activities
- Conversion of existing quizzes into games
- Options to take existing assessments in a competitive environment

The broad aim of gamification is to motivate students to participate in formative assessment by making it fun, but also by focusing them on achieving particular goals. If we get gamification right, games and learning are not parallel processes but closely interrelated; games are completed and won when learning has taken place.

Gamifying lessons with existing (or no) technology

The excitement around gamification might make you feel there is something important that you aren't doing. Actually, many of you will already gamify. You might for example:

- Start lessons with a Kahoot quiz
- Have competitive quizzes or finish lessons with competitive 'leaving tickets'
- Have students amass points for class work or behaviours that translate into team or individual prizes
- Have timed activities in lessons, perhaps with a countdown timer and/or music
- Have role-play activities in which students take on the role of another person

If you aren't doing any of these things, don't panic; the worst that can be happening is that you are missing a trick. Consider whether any of these might work for you, but there is nothing wrong with exercising caution here – game activities need to be congruent and not jarring with the rest of the way you teach.

Dedicated gamification technology

An obvious place to start if you haven't already done so is with Kahoot quizzes. Kahoot's genius has been in taking the simple idea of a competitive multiple-choice quiz and doing it incredibly well; to the student, it is a game; to the teacher, it is a serious formative assessment tool. There are other apps dedicated to gamification, but beware of sites outside the UK and EU that require you to sign up students under their real names – this will probably constitute a GDPR breach.

BookWidgets

One option to consider for gamifying your learning platform is BookWidgets (https://bookwidgets.com). This a commercial product that carries a cost of a few thousand pounds a year for all-teacher access – you pay per teacher, while student accounts are free. The best thing about BookWidgets is that it integrates with MS Teams, Google Classroom or any Virtual

Learning Environment that supports the LTI standard (including Moodle and Canvas). As well as conventional whiteboards, quizzes and flashcards, BookWidgets allows you to create Bingo, Hangman and crosswords.

Moodle games

If you have Moodle, then you have access to a good range of games as a free plug-in. Items from existing quizzes and glossaries can be incorporated into a range of games, including Hangman, Crosswords, Snakes and Ladders and (Who Wants to Be a) Millionaire at the touch of a button. This means that recall of key concepts can be practised numerous times using different games to prevent boredom.

Using technology to prepare for summative assessment

Summative assessment is designed by your Awarding Body, and you will find you have little or no discretion in how you prepare for it. However, preparing students to be assessed is another matter, and you can make a real impact in this area if you use learning technology well. There are many ways to think theoretically about exam preparation, but I find it useful to think of three broad tasks:

- Organising material and imposing a structure on it: If teaching and learning have been optimal throughout a programme of study, this should be quick and straightforward.
- Mastering exam technique
- Memorisation

Note that these are not stages, and all can be interleaved with delivering content. It is not as simple as carrying these out in sequence between delivery and summative assessment.

Concept (and mind) mapping for organisation

Concept maps are potentially useful at any stage in learning, but they are particularly valuable at the beginning of a revision programme when students are trying to impose a structure on the mass of material they need to know. It is often said that effective memorisation always involves testing, and that other activities just waste valuable revision time. I would say that effective memorisation must indeed involve testing, but that it is also helpful for students to have a detailed overview of topics before they start testing. So, provided tools like concept maps or mind maps (the software is essentially the same, although the theoretical roots are very different) are used as well as testing rather than instead of it, they are probably beneficial. Remember that visual mapping techniques do require substantial cognitive activation – they are not the same as just reading through notes.

Mapping tools

There are a number of very good free and paid mapping tools, available both online and as desktop and mobile applications. Online tools have the advantage of making collaboration easy, so you can set group mapping tasks and divide up large tasks like making a class revision plan.

- *Miro*: Miro is an online service with a decent free package and an excellent range of templates. You can work with both traditional mind maps and concept maps, and also flowcharts, workflows and many more.
- *GitMind*: A fairly traditional but well-designed tool with a good free package and a good range of templates, including a useful weekly revision planner! The tool allows for collaboration.
- *Inforapid KnowledgeBase*: This is perhaps the most distinctive and ambitious of all the mapping applications. Like the other tools, it supports mind maps, concept maps and other formats, but it has two killer features: It displays in 3D, and you can import whole documents and web pages to the map. It also includes a revision flashcard tool, so KnowledgeBase can be the foundation of your whole revision programme, not just an organisation tool. Desktop apps cost less than a tenner per user and there is a free online version, though beware that online maps are deleted after 30 days of no use. For €1000 (at the time of writing), you can install an enterprise edition on your own servers. I think this is extraordinary value and definitely worth a look. The interface is more complex than the other tools discussed here, so KnowledgeBase may be best suited to A-level and high-grade GCSE revision.

Revision flash cards

A quite effective student-centred revision strategy involves flash cards; on one side is a question and on the other the answer. Working alone or in pairs, students read the question, attempt to answer it and then turn the card to check their answer. This facilitates recall practice, a well validated memory enhancement technique. This process can be simulated and augmented by various digital flash card generators. Generally, these have an adaptive mode, in which after turning each card students have the option to say that they knew or did not know the answer. Cards reported as answered correctly are then repeated less often than those not reported as answered incorrectly. These are all free, adaptive and well designed:

- *Quizlet*: The original and best-known flash card simulator. This has a huge number of existing shared card-sets to save time.
- *H5P Turning Cards*: By now it won't surprise you to hear that this is my preferred option if you have a VLE – if you don't, the adaptivity feature won't work.
- *LearnItFast*: I really like the interface on this and, like Quizlet, it has a bank of shared card sets. It's perhaps my favourite option if you aren't plugging cards into a VLE.

You have three main options when putting sets of revision cards together: You can use pre-existing sets, make your own or get your students to make their own. Making your own cards is time-consuming, but it has the advantage of answers being reliably correct – and you are able to incorporate the points and examples you used in class (Figure 3.9).

Extended prose preparation

Exam preparation is not just a question of organisation and memorisation. One of the challenges in preparing students for exam assessment is in the skills needed to answer longer questions. Technology can't solve this problem, but a couple of H5P tools might help a bit.

46 Digital assessment

> Question:
> What was Milgram investigating?
> Answer:
> Destructive obedience.
> Check your answer (repeat in):   I WAS RIGHT! (1DAY)   WHOOPS! (5MIN)

Figure 3.9 A LearnItFast card.

- *Structure Strip*: This is an online writing frame that helps you help students structure prose answers. You are provided with a set of writing spaces with pop-up hints. When complete, you copy the structured answer for pasting into a document. Unlike some H5P tools, this one is fully functional even without a VLE.
- *Essay*: This tool allows you write extended prose and receive feedback. It will not accurately assign a numerical mark to a full-length essay, but it is nonetheless extremely useful. Essay can give qualitative feedback based on the wordage and inclusion and exclusion of key words. Because it works on key words, Essay can also provide decent qualitative and quantitative feedback on essay plans; remember, a plan can be in any format the student likes – it just has to include certain concepts. You can also use key word recognition to identify common mistakes in an essay plan. This means students can practice essays and plans and receive meaningful feedback, albeit less complete than what you can provide. This is an example of where technology is nowhere near replacing the teacher but can take some on some of the load and increase what an overworked teacher can reasonably be expected to achieve.

Further information

I've returned to certain themes that constitute ways to improve the effectiveness of assessment a number of times throughout this chapter. One of these is gamification. You can read more about gamification here: https://elearningindustry.com/gamification-for-learning-strategies-and-examples. You can learn more about adaptive learning here – https://educationaltechnology.net/adaptive-learning-what-is-it-what-are-its-benefits-and-how-does-it-work/ – and here – https://www.learninglight.com/adaptive-learning/ – though note that these articles emphasise high-tech applications of hard adaptivity, whereas I have tried to show you simple ways in which to introduce adaptivity and the use of soft adaptivity as well as hard.

Although I have referenced some extremely specialist and brilliantly designed tools in this chapter, I have also returned again and again to H5P as a set of tools to make learning – including assessment – a more interactive process. For a set of H5P/Lumi training resources, try this: https://h5p.org/content-types-and-applications.

4 Digital learning platforms

By the end of this chapter, you should be able to:

- Understand what is meant by learning platforms and Virtual Learning Environments
- Understand what is meant by a walled garden and integration between platforms
- Appreciate the distinction between posts, resources and activities and deploy all on a digital learning platform
- Know a range of platforms of various types and make informed adoption recommendations
- Understand the strengths of the learning platforms you have access to and capitalise on these to maximise engagement
- Design a VLE course so as to boost engagement and learning

Perhaps the first thing to say – especially to experienced teachers and managers who tried and gave up on digital platforms years ago – is that learning platforms have changed beyond recognition and are still in a period of rapid development. So, try not to be put off by bad experiences you might have had a few years ago. The second thing is that the old adage we used to comfort ourselves with – that learning platforms make no impact on learning – has not aged well. You can make a real impact by smart use of one or more modern platforms.

So, you can take it as read that having at least one learning platform at your disposal is an essential weapon in your digital learning arsenal. Why *at least* one? Because there are different types of platforms with different features and strengths, and because some at least will play nicely together. There are many ways to achieve this, but let's start with the basics and look at three categories of learning platform and how they relate to one another.

Broadly, the kind of platforms we can use to deliver, communicate and assess fall into three categories:

1. Cloud-based Office environments
2. External systems based around social streams, quizzes, video etc
3. Virtual Learning Environments

One key point I'm going to make is that you probably shouldn't rely on just one of these categories, so let's make sure you're clear on the language I'm using to describe them.

Base platforms, walled gardens and integrations

In general, regardless of how we use it and what others we might use, we have one main learning platform. We can call this the base platform or base system. Some people rely entirely on this – this is sometimes called the walled garden approach, not to be confused with *Walled Garden*, an Awarding Body's secure website. The alternative to making your base system a walled garden is to link it to additional platforms. This link might be just that – a link, for example from a course page to a quiz or presentation on another site. However, different platforms can be integrated so that an account on one is matched with an account on the other, and users can move seamlessly between the two without additional logins. The mechanism for integrating two platforms is most commonly an API. You won't have to deal directly with APIs unless you work in IT or as a Learning Technologist, but you will hear about them – this is what people mean when they use the term.

What goes on a learning platform?

Your learning platform is only as good as its content. Regardless of the platform you work with, you will be adding three broad categories of content:

- *Posts*: Messages for students – these include instructions, explanations and reminders to ensure that students understand content and are aware of activities and deadlines
- *Resources*: The 'classic' components – documents, presentations and the like
- *Activities*: Tasks that introduce activity and interactivity to students' learning

Resources can be placed on any platform, but although they are sometimes essential, these won't promote engagement. Why would we expect students to get excited about reading a document or presentation – especially one they have seen already? The essence of good platform design is to shift its use from a repository of resources to a site of communication and active learning. Cloud office platforms provide the most straightforward communications tools, while VLEs are king when it comes to providing a wide range of learning activities.

Cloud-based office environments

Virtually all UK schools and colleges use the education versions of MS Office or Google Workspace for communications and file storage. These support simple resources and activities, making it quick and easy to share files, create simple interactives such as forms and assignments, and seamlessly schedule and open live remote lessons. DfE documentation frequently refers to these two as 'learning platforms' so one reason why your Management may emphasise their use because is that it is seen as an expectation. Of course, that expectation grew out of the Covid-19 pandemic, when the primary and urgent need was for a convenient and low-cost way to teach remotely. There is every reason why the education establishment should feel grateful to Microsoft and Google for stepping up as they did, but this is very different to committing long-term to their exclusive use.

Digital learning platforms 49

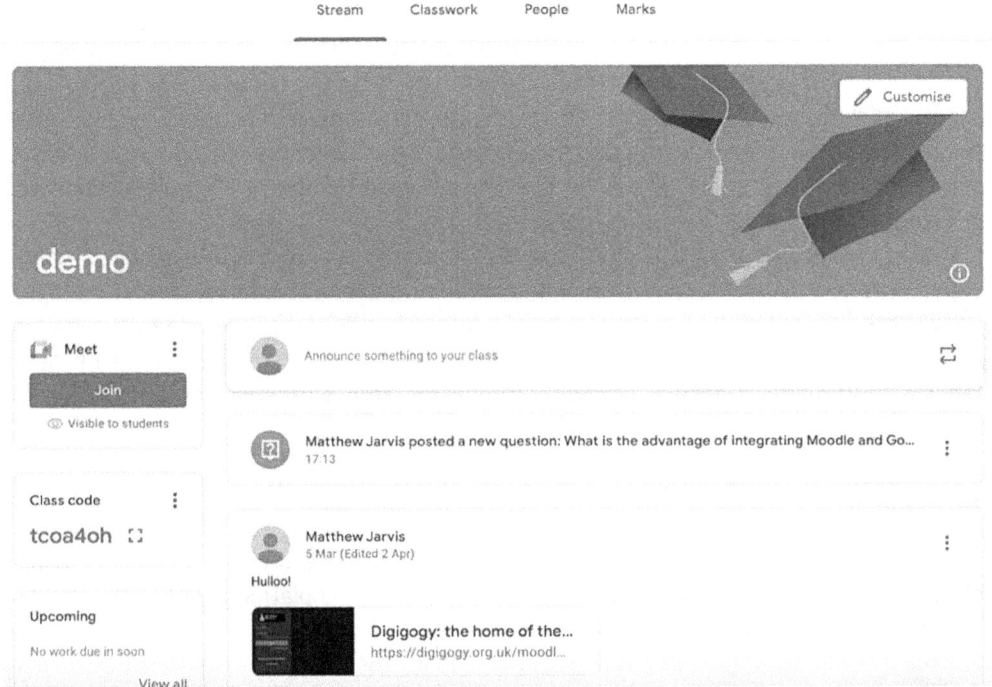

Figure 4.1 The Google™ Classroom interface.

Google Classroom

Of all the learning platforms, Google Classroom has probably made the best impression on students. Consequently, case studies abound of increased student engagement and consequent impact on learning. In fact, the visible impact of Google Classroom is probably responsible in large part for the end of the myth that learning platforms can have no impact on learning. So, what is it, and what does it do?

Google Classroom is primarily an assignment setting, tracking and marking system, but this assessment functionality is set in a simple but attractive social stream, with the ability to set up a Google Meet (see Chapter 5, p. 65) for remote teaching, tutorials or meetings. Each class comes with a Google Drive in which you can quickly create or curate resources like documents and presentations. Quiz functionality is achieved through Google Forms. Being set within Google Workspace, Classroom also gives you and students the ability to create webpages or whole sites, all with a greater degree of oversight than could be provided by using an external site builder.

Google's genius lies not in the range of functionality it provides, but in the quality of design that goes into what it does. Put another way, Google tech doesn't do quite everything you'd like, but what it does, it does really well. This philosophy applies across Google apps, including Classroom.

50 Digital learning platforms

Strengths and limitations of Google Classroom – and a workaround

The greatest strength of Google Classroom is its clean, simple interface and its proven appeal to young people. Its assignment tool is very well designed, for example offering stock feedback phrases (great for time-saving), and It has some unique features like a plagiarism checker that operates at no additional cost. Having a social stream as the main student interface is congruent with the applications students are used to outside formal education and sees a good level of student engagement.

The major limitation of Google Classroom is perhaps the inevitable corollary of its strength – namely, its simplicity. As a way to communicate with students, share static resources and assess work, Classroom is second to none. However, it is pretty limited when it comes to quizzes and entirely lacking in additional interactivity unless you integrate it with other platforms. Fortunately, Google Classroom can be integrated with other platforms, including external commercial platforms and VLEs like Moodle.

MS Teams

Prior to the pandemic and lockdowns, Microsoft played an important role in schools and colleges as a provider of office tools but not really of learning platforms – their Blackboard VLE has long had a presence in the university sector but not so much in schools. However, the Teams business communications platform was rapidly adapted to serve as a learning platform in 2020. Although there have been some tweaks since then, the interface remains essentially the same. Although we often speak of Teams meetings and think of Teams as a remote meeting/teaching tool like Zoom or Google Meet, the meeting tool is set within a wider communications platform that looks and functions a bit like Google Classroom. So, it is probably best to think of Teams as an equivalent and alternative to Google Classroom rather than to Google Meet.

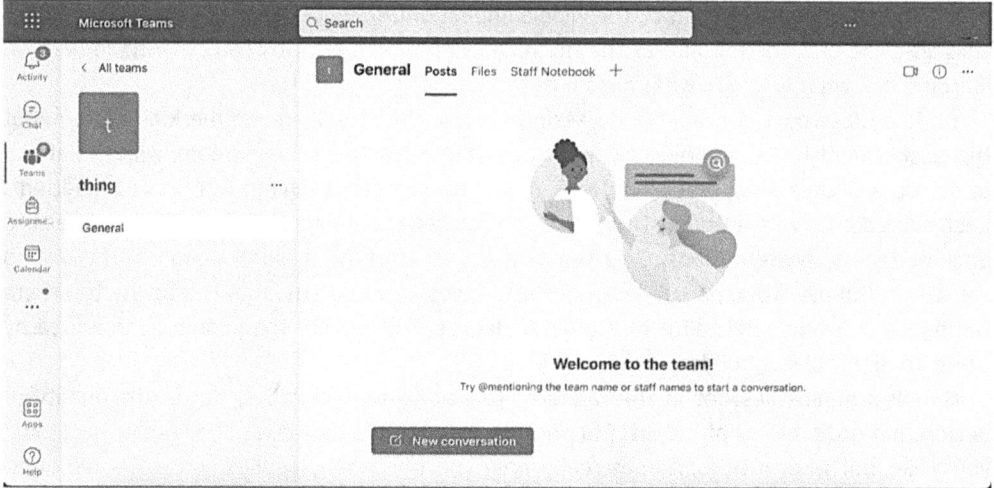

Figure 4.2 The MS Teams interface.

A Teams course is broken down into channels, which can be used for topics or weeks. Remote teaching sessions and meetings are accessed via the small camera icon towards the top left of the page. Chat and assignments are accessed on the left. Teams brings with it all the might of Office 365, so it is arguably the platform of choice for creating and curating documents and presentations. MS Forms provides a comparable, though not identical experience to Google Forms, and can be used to create simple quizzes, the results of which are kept In a gradebook alongside assignment outcomes. The Teams meeting interface is similar to that of Google Meet (both are reviewed in Chapter 6).

Comparing MS Teams and Google Classroom

Teams and Google do roughly the same things, and both have their loyal supporters, so it's not for me to make a recommendation; it just depends on your priorities. Teams was designed as a business tool, and it shows. This appeals to business-minded educationalists, who see the MS Office Suite in general as a valuable acculturation to the business world, and mastery of it as an employability skill. The MS Office Suite unquestionably has the most fully featured word processing and presentation tools around, and OneNote is an excellent tool for handling a range of multimedia in one place. However, development of the education-specific tools like the whiteboard and assignment apps is (at the time of writing) lagging well behind that of Google.

The main weaknesses of the Teams interface lie in its design and workflow. This is obviously subjective, but to me, the Teams page is flawed because with its three columns, it quickly becomes cluttered once there are a number of channels and the social stream is full. There are small icons around the edge of the page, some with quite low figure-background contrast ratios. This is for me a poor design in terms of accessibility, although it should be acknowledged that Microsoft provide an excellent immersive environment (see Chapter 6, p. 86) for their Microsoft Office products, which offers some great accessibility features. Overall, though, the clean and accessible design of Google Classroom wins out for me.

The workflow of Teams also differs slightly from that of Google Classroom. Starting Teams requires that you choose between a fully featured desktop application (a non-starter if you use Chromebooks) and a pared-down web app that opens in your browser. Both are relatively slow to open. This is a minor irritation for most of us but a real problem if you are working with students who struggle with concentration. By contrast, Google Classroom opens quickly in a browser. At the time of writing, the Teams web app lacks some important functionality. The process of adding new topics and resources in Google Classroom is also slightly smoother.

Evaluation of the cloud office approach

Cloud office systems are here to stay, and they provide a convenient way to move between generic technology and simple educational functionality. They have well-designed interfaces and are quite intuitive – staff and students can be quickly instructed in their use.

> **Top tech tip**: Travelling around the country, I often come across assumptions about the relative popularity of MS Teams and Google Classroom. Many people believe that one or the other is 'what everyone is using.' Actually, there are distinct but localised preferences at the level of informal school networks, academy chains and local authorities, so it is easy to get a biased impression according to where you work and who you deal with. In fact, there is no good reason not to have access to both platforms. The basic Google for Education platform is free and upgrades are fairly inexpensive. It also provides some extra useful additional tools like Google Sites and some superior ones like Jamboard, as compared to MS Office. So, if you're a Microsoft-based school or college, it is well worth setting up a Google account as well.

Another reason for the popularity of office suites as learning platforms is that they are effectively free, as your organisation has already paid in order to access email, file storage and word processing and presentation applications. Throw in the fact that office suites are run in the cloud, so all the server-side maintenance work is taken care of for you, and you have an efficient, reliable learning platform with zero direct cost and a shallow learning curve needed to use the system effectively.

So, what's not to like? Well, possibly nothing; it depends on your aspirations for digital learning. If all you plan to do is share documents and presentations, set and mark simple assignments and be able to go remote in response to events that preclude in-person attendance, then your office suite may be all you need. For me – and I accept that I'm biased as a technology enthusiast – that sounds basic and unexciting. So, to conclude, you will need a cloud office system; it could well be your base platform, but it should not be a walled garden. If your organisation sees it that way, they will at some point hit a ceiling in terms of what they can do pedagogically. Integrating with a VLE or one or more external platforms will solve this.

> **Top tech tip**: If your students love the Google Classroom experience, but you also have access to a VLE that gives you a better range of learning activities, get your IT folks to integrate them so you have single sign-on (SSO) between the two platforms. Then you can just post a link to your VLE activity on the Classroom stream. Students won't have to sign in to the second platform or necessarily even be aware they have crossed into it, and activity results will be recorded in the VLE gradebook.

External non-office platforms

Education platforms like Nearpod and Kahoot are no longer one-trick ponies and are increasing their functionality to the point where they could become serious contenders for a school or college's primary learning platform. Some systems that used to be popular in the United Kingdom – Edmodo, for example – do provide a fairly complete service but have fallen by the wayside since GDPR came into effect; remember that storing personal information on US servers is a GDPR no-no. At the time of writing, none of these platforms provide a complete unified package of communications, office tools and education apps, although they may do so in the near future.

For now, the significance of external education platforms is their ability to enhance your existing internal platform. Many external education platforms will integrate with office platforms and/or VLEs. If you use an office platform as your base system, one way to expand its educational functionality is to integrate it with one or more external platforms. Kahoot, Seneca, Nearpod, Quizizz and the like all integrate well with office platforms. Note, however, that this is not a cheap option, particularly as you need several external platforms to provide all the functionality you want.

Virtual Learning Environments

Virtual Learning Environments (VLEs), also called Learning Management Systems (LMSs), are large platforms that can live on your servers or be run by outside providers and delivered as a service. They are content management systems particularly designed for education, meaning that they have elaborate and advanced subsystems for education tasks, particularly in assessment. The best-known VLE platform is Moodle; others include Canvas, Brightspace, Blackboard, Sakai and Frog. Technically, to qualify as a VLE, a learning platform should really conform to a set of common standards. For example, it should accept pre-packaged learning resources in SCORM format and should link to resources or even whole courses in other sites using the LTI (learning tool interoperability) standard. So (at the time of writing) Google Classroom and Microsoft Teams, neither of which adhere to these standards, are *not* VLEs.

At the time of writing, VLEs have fallen out of fashion and, in the school and college sectors (though not in universities), they are often being decommissioned. There are some important things to say about this:

1. VLEs are rarely used to their potential. If you use a VLE for storing documents and presentations, that is massive overkill, and you could achieve the same result more efficiently with your cloud office system. However, you can do so much more with your VLE, including many things that would cost a fortune to buy in as third-party services.
2. Historically, VLE interfaces have often been badly designed, giving students a poor user experience which in turn led to low levels of engagement. We certainly shouldn't downplay the importance of the user experience, but actually there are now many modern VLE themes and, with a bit of thought, this should no longer be an issue.
3. One reason for regarding VLEs as obsolete recently has been the emphasis on remote learning tools. This is actually a misunderstanding of VLE technology, and you have a choice of ways to deliver remote lessons from a VLE, including but not limited to the obvious choices of MS Teams, Zoom and Google Meet.

To summarise, the potential of VLE technology to enhance learning is probably much greater than that of office suites, but so are the challenges of building a well-featured, user-friendly system and engaging users with it. I absolutely recommend having a VLE, but it needs proper planning (see Chapter 7) and investment, including the time of a Learning Technologist, both to build it properly and to train and engage staff.

VLE design: the example of Moodle

There is a huge range of VLEs around, and there isn't space to look at them all. However, we can look in some detail at the most popular and powerful VLE, Moodle. Other VLEs tend to be either offshoots of Moodle or attempts to reproduce it, so you should be able to apply what I say about Moodle to any VLE. Moodle is free and open-source software; however, your school or college will need to pay for hosting and server-side maintenance, so in practice there is a modest cost.

When I carry out Moodle training, the session often begins with a collective groan from delegates who have never seen a well-designed or well-featured Moodle site. Historically, Moodle has often been deployed 'out of the box' with no customisation or staff training. For decades the default Moodle course format was a long column of Word documents and PowerPoint presentations – the so-called 'scroll of death.' The default Moodle theme colours were, until very recently, remarkably ugly. To cap it all, Moodle is a modular system in which all but the most basic functionality comes in the form of plug-ins that have to be added manually to your site. Because Moodle is open-source software and comes without a corporate on-boarding service, many people did not realise this. So, it's no surprise if you have only come across Moodle sites that are functionally limited and ugly as sin! But, all these things can be radically changed with a few hours' input from a Learning Technologist, and a well-designed Moodle site is actually a powerful, versatile and attractive bit of kit.

Moodle appearance

A number of free and commercial themes can be installed in Moodle. These change the colours and other details like font and column width. This might seem like an indulgence, but it can make a massive difference to staff and student engagement – particularly when your site is compared to the brilliantly designed Google Classroom. Your VLE needs to have a modern and attractive feel – see, for example, Figure 4.3.

The course shown in Figure 4.3 is a far cry from the Moodle pages you have probably seen. Colours are modern and attractive, and there is no 'scroll of death' – each topic opens as an accordion when clicked. A weakness of traditional VLE courses is the lack of a social stream, but in this case this is addressed by a 'latest announcements' block at the top of the page. Live remote lessons can be opened directly from the course page, and in fact this is safer than accessing the applications directly because students enter the remote lesson straight from the course page rather than receiving a code that might be shared outside the class.

There are also options to create a completely social course. In the Timeline Course format you post messages and activities rather like in Google Classroom; but the process is faster, and you can draw on a much wider range of activities. See Figure 4.4 for an example.

> **Top tech tip**: The Timeline course format is an excellent communications tool, but it can be hard to find resources and activities shared a few months ago. To avoid this, add an activities block. This file all your activities and resources. As long as you name them appropriately, this makes it easy to find what you want.

Digital learning platforms 55

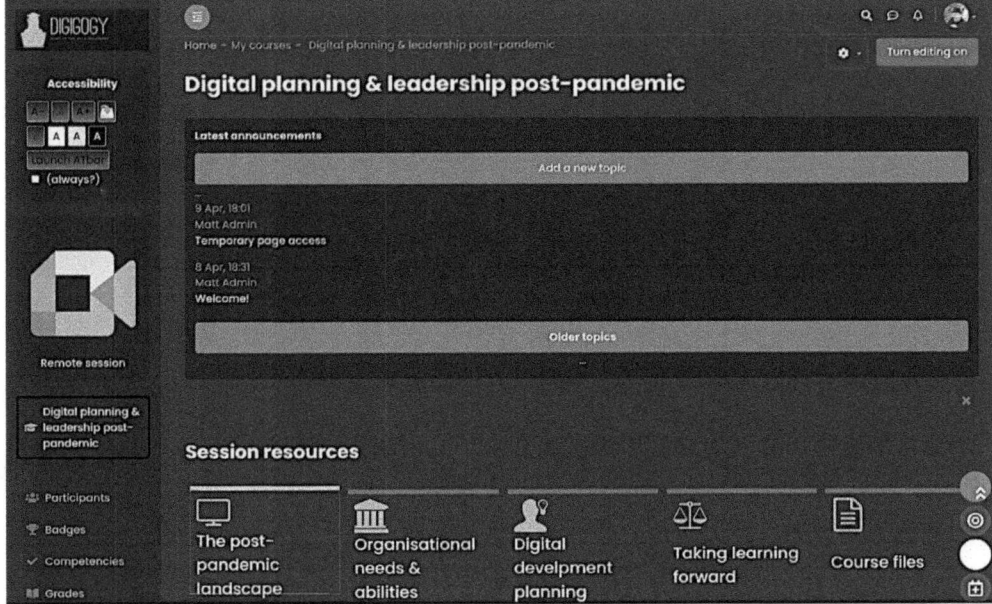

Figure 4.3 A Moodle™ course using the Space theme and Tiles format.

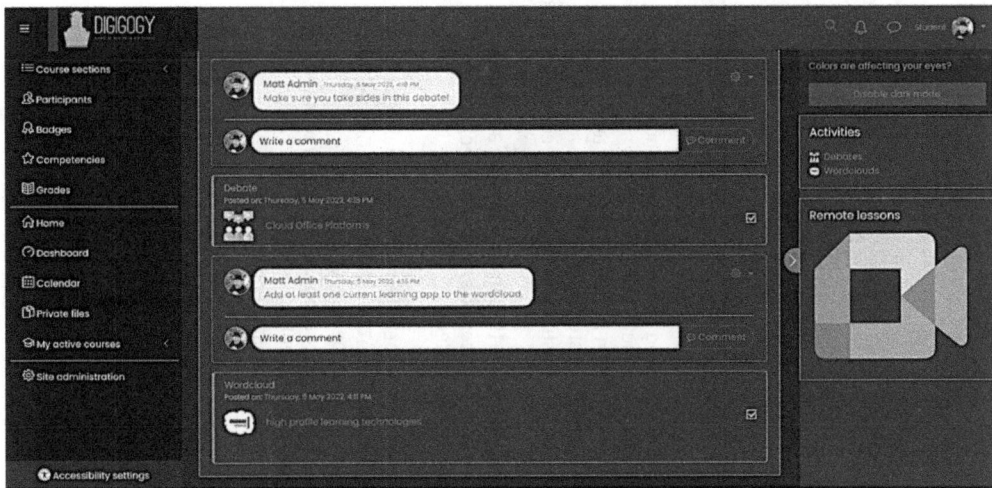

Figure 4.4 The Moodle™ Timeline format.

Moodle activities

Moodle supports a range of free and paid activities – the range of free plug-ins is excellent, going well beyond what others offer. Traditionally, the majority of these have been for asynchronous use, but this is no longer the case. Table 4.1 shows some of the best Moodle activities and their applications.

Table 4.1 Moodle activities

Activity	Purpose	Example use case	Rough equivalent
Assignment	Collection and marking of assigned work, including timed, multiple files and multimedia	Coursework, homework	Google Assignment
Board	Displaying information in blocks, either by teacher or blocks assigned to students	Class collaborative research task presentation	Trello
Checklist	Allowing teachers or students to check off completed tasks	Monitoring project work and multi-part assignments	Checkli
Debate	Allows students to participate in academic arguments	Environmental education	–
Diary	Allows students to record (text, audio, video) and be monitored and graded	Placement monitoring Lockdown monitoring Reflective evidence	Various blogging tools
E-voting	Allows real-time competitive multichoice quizzes and polls	Starter activity	Kahoot, PollAnywhere
External tool	Allows LTI-compliant external objects, e.g. Google Docs and Jamboards to be added	Document sharing, collaborative whiteboard activity	Google Classroom
Feedback	Allows simple student responses, visible to teacher and modifiable by student	Target-setting Self-assessment	Google/MS Forms
Forum	Facilitates assessable student discussions	Encouragement of critical thinking	Google Classroom/Teams
Game	Allows quizzes and glossary items to be converted to games including Snakes and Ladders, Hangman and Millionaire	Starters, plenaries, independent microlearning, revision of key concepts	Flippity
Glossary	Allows teachers and students to define key terms – displayed on course page	Simple microlearning, source of games material	–
Google Assignment	Collection and marking of assigned work	Coursework, homework	Moodle Assignment
Google Meet/MS Teams/Zoom	Fully featured remote teaching/meeting tool	Remote teaching	Meet/Teams/Zoom

Digital learning platforms 57

H5P			
AR scavenger	Allows viewing of VR and AR	Manipulating molecules	–
Audio recording	Allows one-touch recording	Taking notes	Audacity
Cornell notes	Allows note taking from video	YouTube-based homework	–
Course presentation	Interactive presentation tool	Flipped learning	–
Crossword	Allows building of crosswords	Starter, plenary, homework	Crossword Labs
Dialogue cards	Makes adaptive flashcards	Personalised revision	LearnItFast/Quizlet
Dictation	For written answer audio	Literacy/EAL assessment	–
Drag and drop	A kinaesthetic question type	Category/matching tasks	Flippity
Essay	Self-marking short prose tool	Essay planning	–
Interactive book	For making interactive books	Independent/flipped tasks	–
Interactive video	For making video interactive	YouTube-based homework	Vizia
Mark the words	For identifying key words	Deconstructing prose	–
Quiz	Allows multiple question types	General assessment	Quizizz, Kahoot
Sort the paragraphs	Allows putting things in order	BIDMAS, instructions	–
Speak the words	Marks spoken answers	EAL pronunciation	–
Structure strip	For making writing frames	Exam essay preparation	–
Summary	For building retro-organisers	End of topic check	–
Virtual tour	For making 3D interactives	Virtual placement tours	Klapty
Jazzquiz	Allows you to run class quizzes live in competition mode	Starter, plenary, class revision exercises	Kahoot
Notetaker	Allows students to make text or audio notes within courses	Student records bespoke explanation for teacher	OS sticky notes
PDF worksheet	Allows worksheets and workbooks to be completed online and sent to teacher	Any scenario where worksheets and workbooks are used	Amanote
Podcast	Allows teachers/students to record and publish audio or video	Microlearning using short teacher casts	ACast
Sticky Notes	Allows teacher and student to post virtual sticky notes, with optional columns	Brainstorming tasks, sorting tasks	Pinup
Wavefront	Allows 3D models to be displayed	Human anatomy lessons	Sketchfab
Wordcloud	Creates wordclouds in a Moodle course	Brainstorming, starters	Mentimeter/AnswerGarden

Moodle engagement tips

You can see that the broad range of activities in Moodle make it immensely powerful, but there is a downside to this: The sheer range of things you can do with it make Moodle more complicated and harder to learn for staff and students than a simpler platform like Google Classroom. However, there are some strategies to get around this, and the fact that people usually take to simpler environments more quickly is not necessarily a reason to use them – remember, you will hit a glass ceiling of functionality sooner or later in cloud office environments, and if you introduce integrations with third-party sites, you also introduce the same level of complexity as that in Moodle, probably at significantly greater cost.

- Engage staff and students in a co-design process, so that they identify the most useful activities and have a say in the theming and structure of their site. This enhances their sense of ownership over the VLE.
- Recognise that Moodle affords the scroll of death (see Chapter 1, p. 7, for a discussion of affordances), but briefly, it looks like that's how it is meant to be used), and choose course formats that avoid this.
- Be willing to pay for commercial themes that improve the user experience – staff and students will invest more time in learning a system that looks like it provides a premium experience.
- If your Moodle is integrated with Google or Office 365, you can, if you choose, mostly live in those environments and post links to Moodle activities – students never have to use the Moodle environment if they don't like it, and they don't even need to know it exists.
- Create user induction courses for students and teachers and build these into staff and student inductions.
- Use Moodle for fun – e.g. starter quizzes, microlearning homework, etc. – in and out of lessons, right from the start of a course, so that students get to know Moodle and build positive associations.
- Play to the strengths of Moodle and use it primarily to host activities that otherwise wouldn't exist, not just for static files that are easier to share through an office environment. If you aspire only to share handouts and presentations, you don't need a VLE.

Further information

You will probably have picked up on some of my biases in this chapter, but as long as you are making informed choices, there is a range of sound options. If you go primarily down the Google Classroom route, you might find these sites useful:
https://edu.google.com/for-educators/product-guides/classroom/?modal_active=none
https://www.commonsense.org/education/articles/teachers-essential-guide-to-google-classroom

If you or your organisation have opted for the Microsoft approach, you can explore the basics here:

https://www.youtube.com/playlist?list=PLiluTszfwwMJLn1YPlmEW2pnPD1w1j62L

https://www.techlearning.com/how-to/microsoft-teams-tips-and-tricks-for-teachers

For Moodlers and potential Moodlers, try these:

https://www.youtube.com/watch?v=-taoQFZCKTQ

https://moodle.org/

https://learn.moodle.org/

5 Remote teaching

By the end of this chapter, you should be able to:

- Understand the strengths and limitations of synchronous and asynchronous lesson activities and plan a range of blended lesson formats
- Outline some of the major platforms you might use to deliver remote lessons and consider the different opportunities they offer
- Instruct and assess using presentation, video, synchronous quizzes and whiteboards
- Set up and monitor independent learning tasks within lessons, e.g. using social streams, breakout rooms, whiteboards and activity-sequencing tools like Nearpod
- Know etiquette, safety, behaviour management and engagement hacks for remote teaching
- Plan to work effectively with a teaching assistant in remote lessons
- Prepare for particularly difficult remote teaching scenarios
- Take a view on the potential and limitations of remote teaching and plan realistically

This chapter is concerned with delivering lessons remotely. This requires an additional skill set that goes way beyond what is required to enhance conventional teaching by the use of technology. Mass-scale remote teaching is a relatively recent phenomenon, beginning in the UK with the 2020 lockdown. Although teachers and students deserve huge credit for their resilience and flexibility in maintaining lessons on a remote basis throughout lockdowns, claims of a seamless transition to remote learning and uninterrupted learning were massively exaggerated at the time. If it became necessary again to go remote for an extended period, it would be important to implement lessons from this period.

Synchronous, asynchronous and blended lessons

Whole courses, topics and individual lessons can be delivered synchronously, i.e. through real-time interaction, asynchronously, i.e. without real-time comms or blended, i.e. parts of the course or of individual lessons are delivered in real time while others position students in a more independent role. One key to planning successful remote delivery lies in understanding the impact of and balance between synchronous and asynchronous activity.

DOI: 10.4324/9781003266471-5

The policy context

In practice we are constrained in our choices here. During the pandemic, DfE guidance required that online teaching be predominantly 'live,' with an emphasis on teacher-led, whole-class interaction. Other countries may grant more discretion to schools and colleges. Should we undertake wide-scale remote teaching again, there are arguments in favour of the use of both synchronous and asynchronous activities. Let's briefly look at these.

Advantages of synchronous teaching

- There is evidence for broadly better outcomes (not specific to remote teaching) following teacher-led synchronous lessons
- There is clear evidence to show that students prefer at least some synchronous comms, and that interaction in lessons helps maintain engagement and meet students' social needs
- Synchronous comms in lessons allow the teacher to manage behaviour and scaffold understanding in real time as they would in a physical classroom

Disadvantages of (overdoing) synchronous teaching

The assumption that online teaching can and should replicate everything that takes place in the physical classroom has widely been dismissed as naïve, and there is not currently a solid body of research confirming that teacher-led synchronous online lessons consistently lead to better outcomes. In addition, there are some disadvantages to synchronous teaching:

- Whilst the majority of students prefer some live interaction, it may be possible to satisfy this preference with a smaller number of high-quality interactions. Also, it is probably not true for all. Introverts, some students on the autistic spectrum and those who do not wish to reveal their home environment to peers may struggle with or even actively dislike synchronous activity.
- Some students can effectively access lessons only at particular times – for example, if they live in a small, loud environment or one where they have to share hardware. Recorded synchronous sessions are not a like-for-like replacement for properly planned asynchronous lessons.
- Full-time synchronous teaching appears to be significantly more tiring than teaching in a physical classroom and as compared to asynchronous remote teaching.
- The labour-saving in asynchronous teaching is multiplied when lessons are repeated. This is not just a benefit for teachers (though remember that you matter just as much as anyone else in the system), but it means teachers are free to provide bespoke individual support.
- Although asynchronous delivery probably does not require any less preparation time, it will generate resources and activities that can be recycled with parallel classes and in future years. By contrast, plans for synchronous remote lessons will probably be useful only in the event of future lockdowns.

Blended lessons

Of course, you don't have to do pure synchronous or asynchronous teaching, and most of us will blend the two. There is more than one way to skin a cat, and more than one kind of blended lesson. The following taxonomy of blended lessons is loosely adapted from the work of Heather Farmer (2020), who works within the US higher education system.

1. *The flipped lesson*: Asynchronous activity, e.g. watching video, reading, or research, followed by a period of synchronous activity, probably dominated by whole-class interactive teaching. This asynchronous phase can be carried out before or during the formal lesson time and is intended to develop skills of independent study and maximise the productivity of synchronous interaction. To be effective this requires a really clear brief, some degree (depending on your students) of monitoring during the asynchronous phase and a well-planned and actioned synchronous phase.
2. *The concept mastery lesson*: The classic one-idea-per-lesson structure, in which you begin with synchronous delivery of the essentials, for example using video or presentation applications. After this, students complete some independent or collaborative tasks to consolidate their understanding, and you wrap up with a plenary. This probably works best for subjects that break down to clearly identifiable chunks of content or distinct skills, and won't be of much use for ongoing art projects.
3. *The bootcamp lesson*: This is a more intensive variation on the previous lesson type, in which the teacher leads students through a rapid sequence of activities, some teacher-led and others more independent – perhaps involving peer collaboration in breakout rooms. This kind of lesson may be most effective for shorter lessons with students that may struggle to stay motivated in a less structured environment. It requires more elaborate preparation and more intensive teacher effort than the others, so it is best targeted selectively according to student need. Overuse of bootcamp lessons may inhibit student autonomy and leave you burnt out.
4. *The monitored project lesson*: Apart from a starter and plenary, students work independently at their own pace on a project, with you present throughout in a monitoring and scaffolding role. Project-planning, synchronous tutorial and checklist monitoring tools can really help make this kind of lesson work smoothly, as they allow you to monitor progress without constant switches of attention. This allows you and students to set your own pace with time for individual help. You should be less tired after this kind of lesson than after a more teacher-intensive lesson provided you have laid the groundwork so that students can be fairly autonomous.
5. *The autonomous project lesson*: This is a variation on the monitored project lesson, in which you step back a bit more and allow students to work more autonomously. This probably works best with more advanced and experienced students who have experience with monitored project lessons. Remember that, as students are self-regulating for most of the lesson, it becomes particularly important in autonomous project lessons for you to rigorously assess their engagement and progress. The risk with this type of lesson is that those who disengage may remain disengaged for some time before you notice.

> **Top tech tip**: It's worth trying all five of these lesson formats and switching between them, but as a default it might be worth starting topics with concept mastery lessons. Recall the expertise reversal effect (see the 'Cognitive load theory' section of Chapter 1, p. 8-9); students are initially advantaged by direct instruction when they lack expertise in an area, but as they learn more, the advantage tends to shift to more student-centred methods. Concept mastery lessons allow for expertise reversal. Once a topic is underway and students have a basic understanding, you can probably vary lesson formats.

Webinars vs whole-class interactive lessons

The synchronous element of remote teaching can vary on another dimension – the extent of interaction. At one extreme, webinar lessons do not allow any interaction; students can simply see and hear the teacher. At the other end of the spectrum, all students can see and message each other as a whole class and in breakout rooms.

You can to some extent control what students can see; exactly what you can control and how depends both on what tool you are using and the account your school or college has with the provider. For example, in Google Meet you can prevent chatting and screen-sharing and you can instruct students to use a use Spotlight view rather than a grid, but you cannot (at the time of writing) prevent students from seeing each other.

Some applications, such as Zoom, allow you to control whether participants are visible at the start of a lesson, and Zoom permits a webinar mode where attendees cannot interact at all; but for safeguarding reasons, you won't generally have control over student webcams.

The NSPCC has recommended using a webinar format in order to meet the needs of more vulnerable learners who may not enjoy interacting online. However, not all platforms permit pure webinar lessons. It is worth bearing in mind, though, the principle that lesson formats with less interaction are safer and less intimidating for vulnerable learners. Generally, the more interaction you permit, the greater the potential (though not necessarily the reality) for learning and for remote lessons to meet social needs, but also the greater the potential for behaviour management and safeguarding headaches. Perhaps the most important lessons from this debate are:

- Plan the level of interaction with the needs of the particular students in mind
- Know how to quickly change the level of interaction in response to how a lesson is going

Technology for remote teaching

As an individual teacher you may well have no choice about which tool you use, but many of you will have access to more than one option – and of course, you *may* be in a position to influence choice of platform. Note that if your institution has Microsoft and Google accounts and a VLE, then you probably have a range of good options.

64 Remote teaching

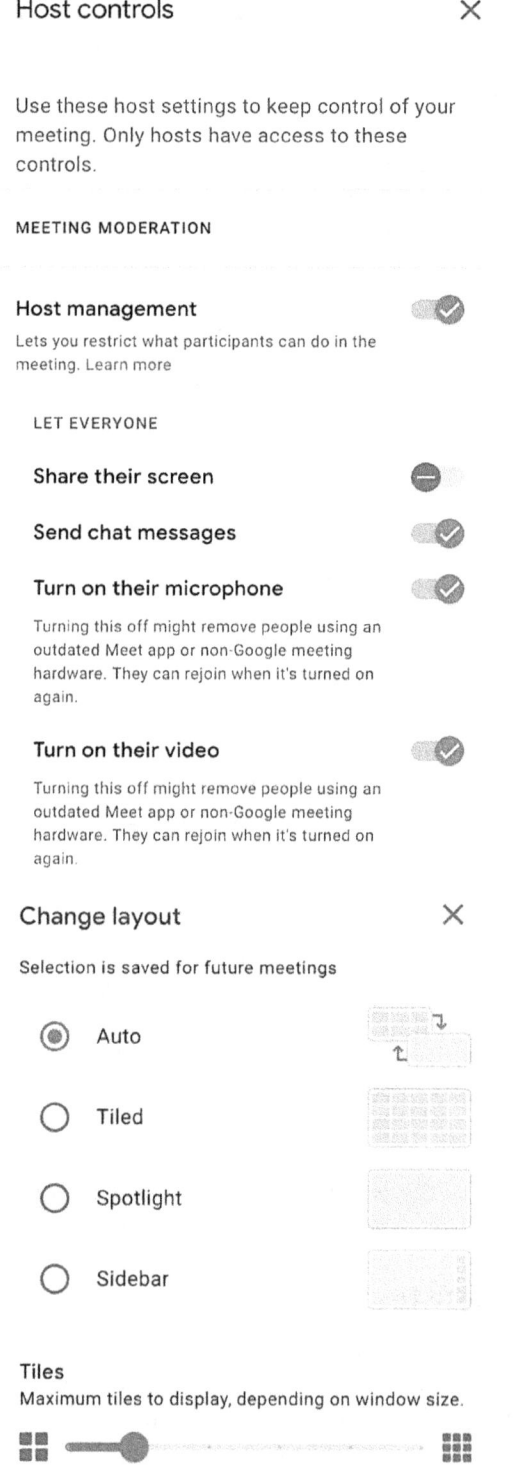

Figure 5.1 (a) The Google™ Meet host controls; (b) Google™ Meet view controls.

The policy context

Most DfE documentation references Google and Microsoft platforms, and there are sound reasons for this; if you and colleagues are already familiar with Office 365 or Google Workspace, then introducing MS Teams or Google Meet will entail a shallow learning curve and need not entail any extra cost. However, there is no compunction to use these platforms, and there is a good range of options out there.

Google Meet

This is probably the most intuitive remote teaching app to use, and it is popular with students. It can be found in the Google Workspace (the 'waffle' at the top right of your Chrome browser window). When you select it, you have the choice of joining an invited meeting or creating a new one. This can be instant or calendared.

> **Top tech tip**: Before you join a Google Meet, do check that you are still logged into the right account – Google technology has the annoying habit of reverting back to a default account whenever you change a page. So, if you use your personal and work Google accounts on the same machine or sync browsers across machines, you can easily find yourself logged into a lesson with your personal account. This is a potentially serious safeguarding and data protection risk, especially if you record lessons. Try Google Chrome profiles to avoid this.

Google Meet provides the essential meeting tools in a very intuitive interface. In all versions you can change or blur your background, raise a hand, present a browser tab or desktop application, change view to see your class or focus on a speaker and open a file or whiteboard. The Google Jamboard is a particularly well-designed interactive whiteboard, both intuitive to use and well featured.

If you are working on a desktop or laptop, then your Meet will open in a browser tab. Teachers who like to have multiple browser windows and tabs open can find that they lose track of their Meet tab. However, in contrast to MS Teams (at the time of writing), this means that all functionality is accessible from the browser – this is important if you don't have access to a desktop app.

At the time of writing there are some limitations to the capabilities of Google Meet in the free version of Google Workspace. In particular, there is no facility to open breakout rooms. There are various browser plug-ins that can simulate breakout rooms; however, the experience is not the same as the native capability. More importantly, before you install one of these, be sure to check it for data protection. Anything external that can access student details without particular safeguards will constitute a GDPR breach.

66 *Remote teaching*

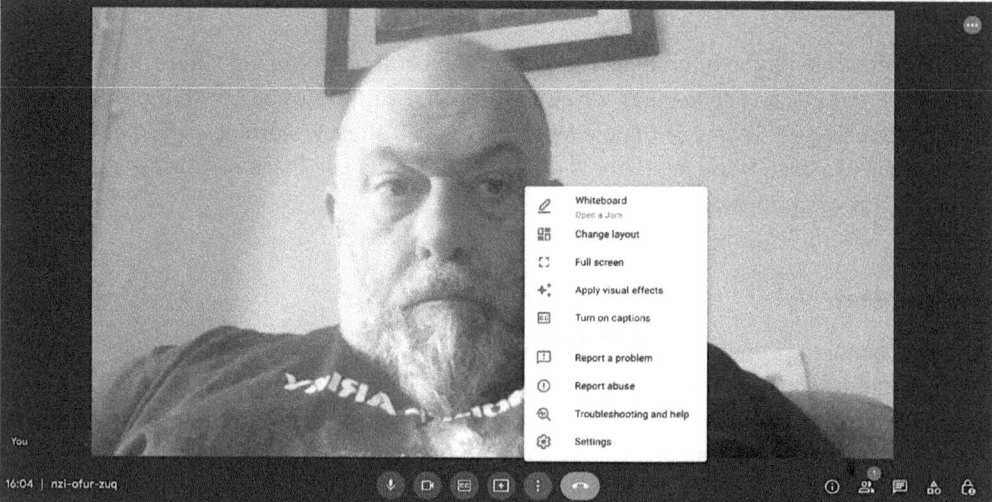

Figure 5.2 The Google™ Meet controls.

Microsoft Teams

Although Teams and Meet are popular alternatives, they do not provide a like-for-like experience, and each system has its own advantages and disadvantages. I use both, and I'm not going to try to sway you one way or the other. That's not a cop-out or fear of litigation! They genuinely are different, and each has their loyal supporters.

The first difference with Teams is that the remote teaching application sits within a wider Teams communications application in which you can post messages, chat and set and mark work. Of course, Google tech allows you to do all these things, but they are not integrated into the same application. So, Teams is not just a remote live teaching application but a shot at something much more ambitious.

This sounds like an advantage – and it *can* be, *if* you plan to use all this functionality, and *especially if* you don't already have that functionality elsewhere. However, the comprehensive nature of Teams can also be a drawback. Generally, you require more clicks and a considerably longer initialisation time when starting or joining a Teams lesson than is true for alternatives. This is only mildly annoying for most, but it can present real problems for students with concentration or memory problems. Also, if you have an existing VLE, it can become non-obvious where different tasks should be carried out (I have a couple of solutions for this; see Chapter 4).

Another issue is that Teams looks like a business tool – because essentially, it is! This in itself is a bonus and a problem. Because Teams is a standard business tool, acculturating students to its use provides them with an 'easy hit' employability skill. On the other hand, the business look can be a real turn-off for some students. I recently heard one student comment that Teams was 'like something my Dad would use.'

The functionality of the Teams desktop meeting application is broadly similar to that of Google Meet. You have the usual ability to change background, raise a hand, see different views, share screen and chat. You have access to a rather more basic whiteboard than Google's offering, but you do get breakout rooms.

> **Top tech tip**: The Teams web app (at the time of writing) has much more limited abilities than the standalone app. You can't change or blur background or open breakout rooms. Critically, if accessibility is a priority for your organisation (remember, if you are an FE College or Private Training Provider, it is a legal requirement), you can't display captions. If you use Chromebooks and don't have the option of a desktop app, this is particularly problematic. As long as the web app has this restricted functionality, I would avoid it and avoid Teams altogether if you use Chromebooks. This is likely to change during the life of this book.

Figure 5.3 (a) The Teams Meeting web interface; (b) The Teams app interface. Microsoft Teams is a trademark of Microsoft.

Zoom

Zoom was perhaps *the* great technology success story of the 2020 lockdown, with 29 million downloads in one single week. The 40-minute free personal version and the good-value licenced version with unlimited meeting time proved deservedly popular. The thing to know about Zoom is that it operates according to a very different business model from that of Meet or Teams. Where personal accounts represent great value, organisational licences are much more expensive, and your school or college may well have not invested. I wouldn't want to oversimplify the decision about whether to invest in Zoom by offering generic advice here: Zoom *is* in some ways a superior experience. But whether it is superior *enough* to justify many additional thousands of pounds a year is one for your school or college to decide.

If your school or college has invested in a Zoom account, then great – there is no question that it provides an excellent user experience. The critical thing to know as a teacher is *not* to use a personal account for teaching purposes. This would constitute a serious data protection and safeguarding issue, especially if you record lessons.

In the 2020 lockdown, Zoom received some bad publicity over security and safeguarding issues. Nowadays, Zoom is intrinsically no less safe in its design than alternatives, although extra effort has been made by hackers to work out ways to hack into Zoom meetings – so-called 'zoom-bombing.' This isn't Zoom's fault, but it does mean you probably should be extra vigilant when it comes to security and safeguarding when using Zoom.

VLE plug-ins

Meet, Teams and Zoom all plug into popular VLE platforms like Moodle, Canvas and Blackboard. These platforms also provide access to other video-conferencing tools. Although we often think of our VLE as a dated file store, it is actually far more than that, and it will support live remote teaching just as well as online office suites and standalone conferencing tools.

There are advantages to using the VLE as a remote teaching application. You can display files and interactive content from the same page without logging into separate environments, and in general, students will need fewer clicks in a more accessible environment to navigate to their lesson.

If you are thinking of delivering remote teaching in your VLE, there are other tools you can use to run live lessons. One such is BigBlueButton (BBB), which integrates into Moodle, Canvas and Sakai VLEs. If your institution has a dedicated server available, and either the necessary in-house expertise or a few hundred pounds to pay for installation, BBB arguably provides the best overall experience for teachers and students of any remote teaching application. Picture quality and lip-syncing are flawless, and there are a range of distinctive features such as built-in polling and real-time slide annotation.

Tools and techniques to aid live instruction

Recall J. J. Gibson's idea of affordances (see the 'Affordances' section of Chapter 1, p. 7). In the same way that PowerPoint looks like a tool for presenting endless bullet points and Moodle looks like a platform to list endless presentations and handouts in a scroll of death, Teams, Meet, Zoom and the like *look* like tools to allow you to talk to your students. This means

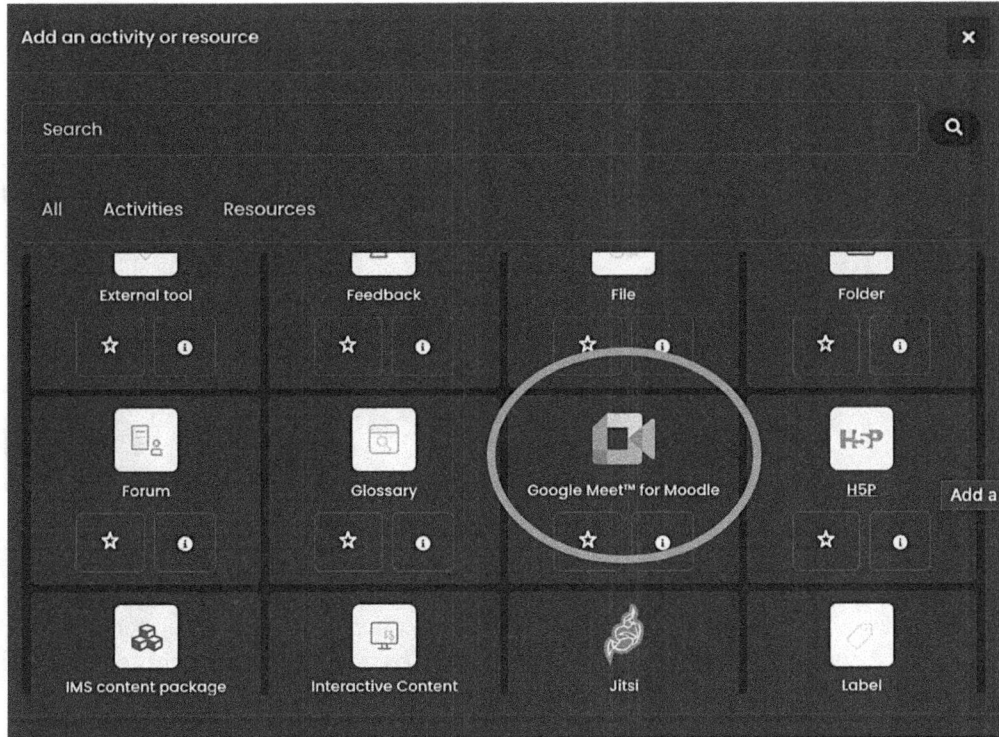
(a)

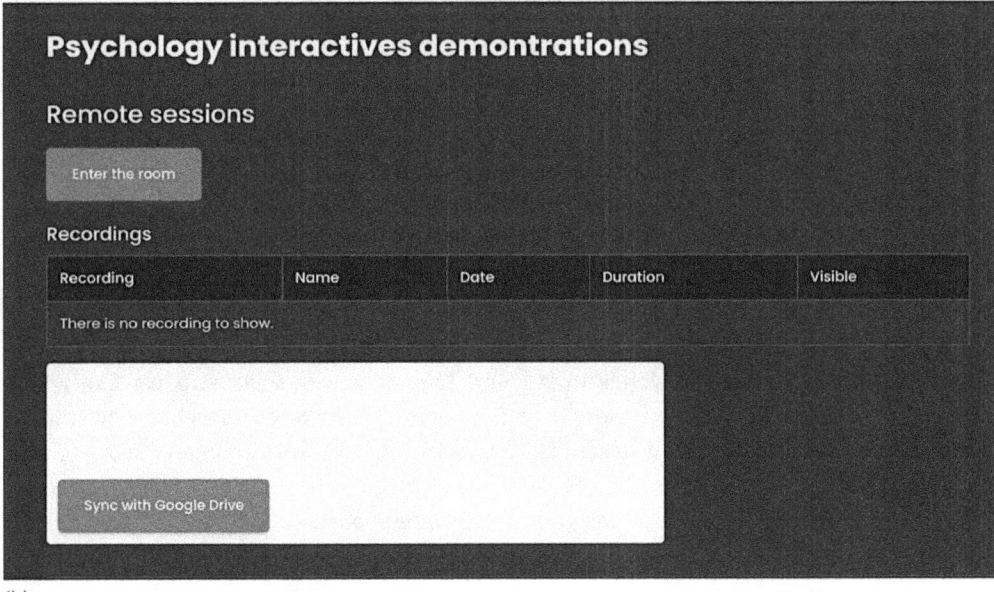
(b)

Figure 5.4 (a) The Moodle™ add an activity interface with Meet selected (b) Adding a Google™ Meet to a Moodle™ course: configuring the Meet.

Figure 5.5 The Big Blue Button interface.

that, unless you take a step back and plan carefully, it is very likely that you will find yourself mostly talking in live remote lessons. Unless you have Churchillian skills of oratory, the last thing you should do is mostly talk at your students! That means you will want to make the best use of the pedagogical tools available. The following are built into all the major systems:

Social streams

You'll need a way to communicate the details of tasks in writing as well as in virtual person – it's unrealistic to expect all your students to retain all the details of complex verbal instructions. Probably the most convenient way to do this is with a social media-style stream. If you have access to a course stream, I recommend using it and not putting instructions – at least not initial instructions – on attached documents. The extra click and short delay while opening a document are much more off-putting than you might expect if you haven't observed the reactions to both options. Remember as well that most young people find email an outdated technology and avoid it wherever possible, so that is usually a poor medium for delivering instructions. Social streams can be found in Google Classroom, Microsoft Teams and the Moodle Timeline course format (more of that in Chapter 3).

It is worth considering how you want students to engage with social streams. Every time you encourage social interaction, there is both an opportunity for co-operative learning and a risk of conflict, bullying and distraction. You know your students and can make the best decisions here, but whatever you decide, make sure you know how to control when students can interact and how to remove offensive or inappropriate posts (while preserving evidence).

Presentation/screenshare

This has different titles in different applications, but in general you will have an option to present files, browser tabs or your whole desktop from your meeting. So, if you start a particular conventional lesson with an online quiz, say a Kahoot, followed by a PowerPoint or

Google Slides presentation and a YouTube video, you can replicate this sequence of activities in your remote lesson. Have your quiz open on one tab, your video on another and your presentation either on a further browser tab or a desktop application depending on how you like to deliver presentations and use the browser tab and/or 'window' option on your present tool.

> **Top tech tip**: In MS Teams you have the additional option to run PowerPoint presentations directly from within Teams. This gives you the ability to decide whether students can move through slides ahead of you. If you do this, make sure that you have pre-loaded the PowerPoint you want to use in advance of the lesson and that it shows up in your share tray. This can be a bit buggy.

Whiteboard

All the major remote teaching apps allow you to present an interactive whiteboard during lessons. Crucially, you can make this collaborative or keep it under your control alone. Give this some thought before the lesson, but also bear in mind that you can change the collaboration settings during the lesson. The procedure for this is different for each app, so make sure you know how to change sharing settings on your application.

You don't have to stick to the built-in whiteboard applications, although there are some good reasons for doing so. Both the Microsoft Whiteboard and Google Jamboard have really excellent kinetics – so although it's always going to be hard to write freehand using a mouse this can be harder on third party apps. Also, you have the option of typing text on both. The main limitation of all the built-in whiteboards in the standard teaching apps is the inability to view and annotate a file. You can work around this by using a different annotation tool or by setting a picture of the file you want to annotate as the background or pasting text into a textbox.

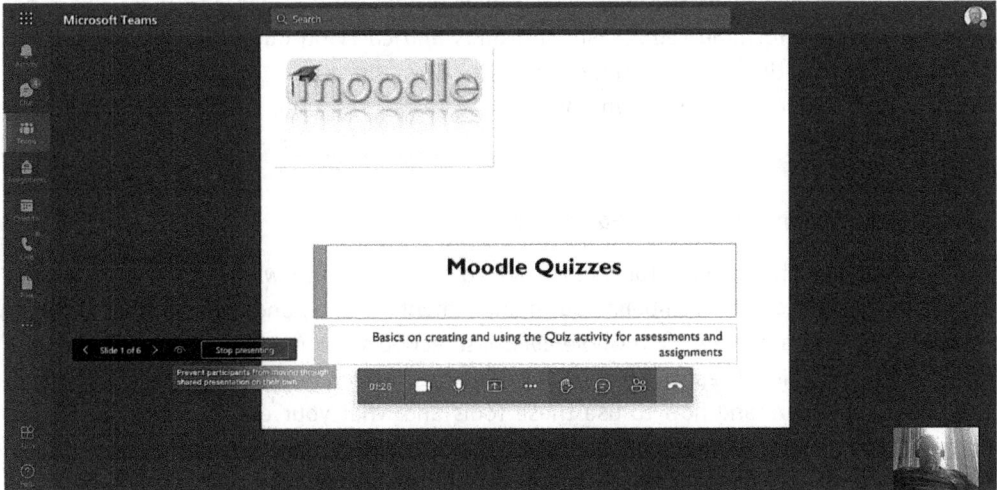

Figure 5.6 Presenting a PowerPoint from within a Teams meeting.

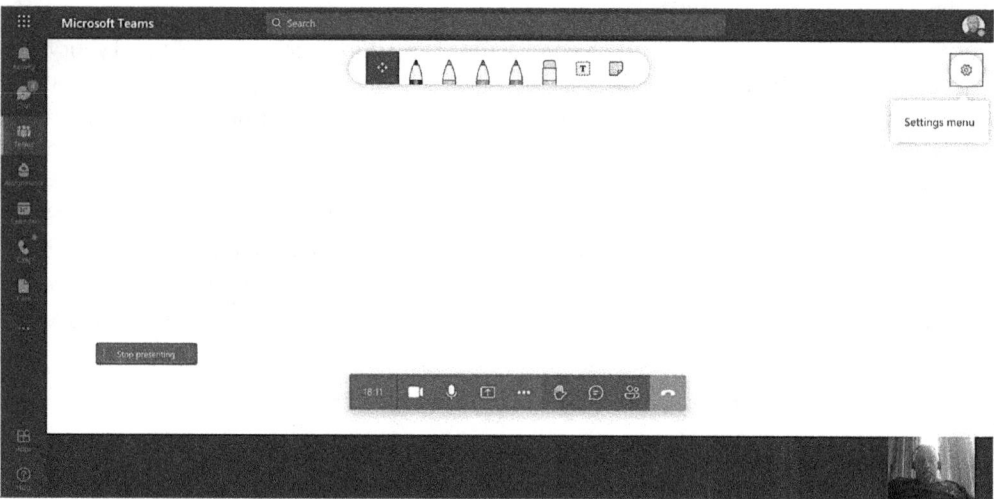

Figure 5.7 The MS Teams whiteboard.

Breakout rooms

All the major remote teaching applications support breakout rooms, subject to your licence, and, in the case of MS Teams, using the standalone app. The idea of breakout rooms in the education context is to simulate the standard practice of grouping students and giving them a collaborative task. At the time of writing, breakout rooms are fairly new and the response of many students has been surprisingly ambivalent. As one student put it: 'It's so awkward. They put you with random people and just expect you to talk!'

It seems, then, that at least some students find breakout rooms with peers they don't know well an intimidating experience – much more so than the superficially similar situation of sitting around a table in a physical classroom. One obvious way to mitigate this is to ensure that students are grouped with friends or familiar classmates. Where this is not possible, consider forming regular small groups and carrying out ice-breaker exercises. Also consider creating a group structure with tasks allocated – this may help shift the focus of each student to their own contribution rather than the social ambiguity of the situation.

Social interactions: chat and hands-up

The standard remote teaching tools come with a chat function – which you should be able to turn on and off to help with behaviour management – and a hands-up icon that students can use to answer a question in a whole-class interactive session and summon help in more independent activities. These are technically pretty self-explanatory; my main tip is to ensure that students understand how to use these tools and what your expectations are around their use. For example, if you don't want peer-to-peer chatting but do want to leave chat on for questions, this needs to be clearly communicated. This is a behaviour management issue rather than a technical one.

Session recording

All the major remote teaching tools allow you to record at the touch of a button. Although many schools and colleges record all lessons as a matter of course, this raises a number of nuanced issues, and I would give it some careful thought.

- Posting recorded lessons presents students who can't be at live sessions with an opportunity to see, though not participate in, that lesson. Is this the best way to help them catch up? Pragmatically it might be the best you can do, but I would be wary of assuming you've done all you'd like to do for a student by posting a recording.
- Are all the students comfortable with being recorded? This is an ethical issue, with more introverted and otherwise vulnerable students often not wishing to participate in a recorded session. It might also be that students living in visibly impoverished or chaotic surroundings are uncomfortable to have cameras on and their homes recorded.
- What else might recorded lessons be used for? It is probably not controversial to review recorded lessons for safeguarding purposes, but what about quality assurance? Past research into the recording of conventional classrooms for observation purposes has shown that teachers were fairly comfortable with being recorded, *provided that they had control over what was recorded and what happened to the recording*. So, there is a world of difference between a teacher choosing to record a lesson and share it, and a quality assurance system that samples retrospectively from a bank of recorded lessons. It may well also be a data protection offence to use a recording for a different purpose to that it was obtained for.

Depending on the nature of your students, you might be swayed by the different ways in which remote teaching applications handle recordings. Zoom saves them on your allocated webspace or your hard drive - fine for an institutional account or machine, not fine for your personal account or hardware. Google saves to your Google Drive - again, no problem as long as you are using an institutional Google account.

Teams (at the time of writing) handles recordings differently unless you pay for an upgrade. Recordings are available to students in the message dialogue. Whilst this saves you a few clicks in sharing, it also means that if something inappropriate happens in a lesson, such as an uninvited guest sharing pornography - or much worse, 'revenge porn' featuring a class member (hideous, I know, but it happens) - students can all obtain a copy. You know your students and whether this is a likely scenario.

Other apps to use in live remote teaching

There are thousands of apps you might find useful, but these are some of the most popular and exciting:

- *Kahoot*: Kahoot in its own right is discussed in detail in Chapter 3. As regards remote teaching, Kahoot now integrates with Meet, Teams and Zoom, meaning you can easily use the charming quiz tool with the enormous bank of time-saving existing quizzes in your lessons.

- *Nearpod*: Nearpod can be seen as a VLE substitute, but this probably does both Nearpod and VLEs a disservice. What Nearpod does really well is allow you to access a huge range of good-quality existing activities (though these are mapped on to the US curriculum, not the UK curriculum) and sequence activities into a lesson, or perhaps a more student-centred chunk of a lesson. This doesn't have to be a remote lesson, but Nearpod comes into its own when you use it remotely. Nearpod now integrates with Microsoft, Google and Zoom platforms – and into VLEs like Moodle.
- *Moodle*: Everything you can do in Kahoot and Nearpod you can do in Moodle, and much more, provided you have the right plug-ins. Moodle requires a few more clicks to do things and the learning curve is steeper, but its breadth of functionality is impressive. Moodle does integrate with Microsoft, Google and Zoom platforms, but the user experience is different, being based in a Moodle course (except Teams, where you can 'live' in either the Teams or the Moodle environment).
- *Lumi*: The most exciting interactive features in Moodle now come from a plug-in that enables the incredible H5P software (discussed in detail in Chapters 3 and 4). There is now a way to freely make and access H5P online without Moodle - the Lumi project. Lumi has been around as a desktop app for a while but it is now also available as an online platform. You can set up a free account at https://app.lumi.education/ .

Remote teaching lifehacks

This final section is all about ways to make your life – and those of your students and colleagues – easier while delivering remote lessons.

Planning safe and managed lessons

We will revisit safeguarding remote lessons in detail in Chapter 6, but in brief, you need to be aware of student behaviour and the extra risks to student well-being of using remote teaching technology and plan accordingly. We have already come across the risks of recording and the complex issues around webcams. It is generally a good idea to limit the ability of students to access remote lessons before you and to interact at will.

Access to interactive features

For most classes it's probably not necessary to disable all interaction features entirely (although you know best how risky they might be in your particular context), but you probably want to ensure that students can't access a lesson before you, admit non-students to lessons or share screens unless directed to do so. The mechanics of how to do this differ between platforms, so make sure *you* know how to do it, and don't assume that if you move platforms, the process will be the same.

Most of the time it's a good idea to allow only people with an institutional email into lessons – and teams, in the case of MS Teams – in order to eliminate 'zoom-bombers.' However, you might want to reconsider this if you have parents who want to help students during remote lessons. That is a valuable opportunity that I would really want to enable. You may find this option controlled in admin settings, so discuss it with your administrator if the default settings don't suit you.

Breakout rooms
Breakout rooms present additional safeguarding and behaviour management risks in remote lessons, as you can't simultaneously monitor several of them, and as many students feel vulnerable in them. Again, you probably don't need to throw out the idea of breakout rooms; just use them with an awareness of the possible risks to your particular students.

Setting expectations
Remember that remote lessons are a unique experience, and that it may not be obvious what constitutes appropriate behaviour. It follows, then, that if you want students to stick to particular behaviours, you might need to make them very clear. For example, if you are explaining something and you want quiet except for clarification questions, tell your students that the appropriate way to get your attention is through the 'hand-up' button. It's not a bad idea to share or negotiate virtual class rules when you start remote teaching.

Sanctions
You have some sanctions available to you in live remote lessons. Most obviously, you can mute disruptive students or move them to the waiting room. Before you do the latter, make sure you know the capabilities of your application. For example, in the free version of Google Meet, you can't (at the time of writing) re-admit someone once they are removed from a lesson.

At the school/college level
Clearly, safeguarding and behaviour management do not operate just at the level of the individual teacher and class. The following ideas have either proved helpful already, or are lessons learned from the 2020-21 lockdown:

- Make sure someone has training in e-safety, e.g. that provided by the National Crime Agency, and that they are available for teachers to consult. This might be a designated safeguarding officer or Learning Technologist – ideally both.
- Publish a policy for safe and well-managed lessons so that teachers and students are aware of conventions, advice and sanctions before they engage in remote teaching. Supplement his with a simple, easy-to-remember, poster-style set of rules for students.
- Where a lockdown looks likely, e.g. at the start of a future pandemic, introduce a blended delivery model so that teachers and students get used to remote teaching before it becomes the dominant delivery mode.
- Consider the welfare of teachers who engage in long hours of remote teaching and avoid prescribing a rigid model of delivery that puts teachers at risk of burnout.

Etiquette and consideration in remote lessons

There is clearly a huge overlap between etiquette and behaviour management. Your demeanour sets the emotional and behavioural tone for a lesson. The following tips are some obvious and non-obvious examples of etiquette tips.

- Model courtesy and respect in your communication – just as you would in a physical classroom.
- Punctuality is just as important in virtual lessons, as students won't be able to access the lesson until you start it – and may start grumpy after waiting.
- Encourage students to dress in a way that won't distract others. Also, encourage them to avoid wearing stripes or other strong patterns, as this can affect video quality.
- Avoid multitasking when your camera is on, as this can look inattentive and thus signal disrespect. It is better to turn your camera and microphone off for a time when learners have been set a substantial task and you are resting your eyes and stretching your legs.
- Tell students when you want them to work independently and, if you are taking a break, when you will be available. Don't take a break as soon as you set a task as there will virtually always be some initial questions.
- Mute your microphone when not speaking – any noise at your end, like yawning, coughing and finger tapping, are *much* louder across an internet connection than in a conventional classroom!

Engagement hacks

Once again, this overlaps with previous categories of lifehack, but I would consider these strategies from the perspective of keeping students engaged in remote learning.

- Consider the emotional tone of your delivery. Too flat, and you risk boring students. Less obviously but equally problematic, too-lively delivery may overstimulate students with autistic characteristics and those with ADHD and emotional-behavioural problems.
- Be realistic about how long you will keep students' attention and keep critical lesson content within that parameter. You almost certainly won't keep students' full attention for as long as you would in a conventional classroom, so you may have to be more focused in your learning outcomes.
- Balance synchronous and asynchronous activity and provide some synchronous support in asynchronous activities. As already discussed (Chapter 2, p. 22), you are unlikely to keep students' attention if you talk too much, but equally, students may not feel held in mind if you withdraw completely from a lesson and leave them to get on without support. Project-planning tools and checklists can help you and students keep focused and up to speed in more independent work, and monitoring these can be a low-stress way to keep track of progress. Be aware, though, that these tools do require some advance set-up and training.
- There are a range of tools that aim to improve engagement, but be aware that you need to use a range and not overuse any single app. By the end of the 2021 lockdown, an awful lot of students were bored with Kahoot – excellent tool though it is.

- Don't forget subject-specific and subject-oriented technology (explored in more detail in Chapter 3). In the drive to master Teams, Meet, Zoom and the applications that neatly plug into them, many of us lost the habit of using subject-based tech like we use regularly in the physical classroom. One way to keep it fresh and relevant is to re-focus on sharing subject-based tech through remote applications.
- Capitalise on the opportunity to develop student creativity and independent learning. This may be most useful if you aren't teaching a cohort in an exam year, but it can also be a radical way to rethink your planning in any situation. While you probably won't deliver the same volume of information effectively whilst engaged in remote teaching and learning, you may be able to foster the development of some different skills such as working independently and creatively. For example, students could take responsibility for an area of the curriculum, building a collaborative website or wiki. This may prove a less efficient use of time than teacher-led instruction in a conventional classroom, but you can overcome the worst of this by effective assessment and by providing an initial grounding in the topic – recall the expertise reversal effect from Chapter 1. And remember, your comparator is not the physical classroom but a different model of remote delivery, so you may not lose as much as you expect. It's worth a thought, anyway.

Remember your teaching assistant!

If you are lucky enough to have a teaching assistant (TA) or learning support assistant (LSA) in your remote lessons, it is worth planning with them in mind. Often, the funding for their posts is tied to the needs of particular students, so you probably won't be entirely free to deploy them across a group as you would like. However, you should still include them in your planning, and bear in mind that at least some students who need TA support will benefit from *some* autonomous time in lessons. The following tips may be useful:

- This will be egg-sucking for experienced teachers, and of course it applies to conventional teaching just as much as remote: Make time to brief your TA on the structure and content of a lesson and discuss the implications of the tasks for the student(s) they are working with.
- Give the TA teacher-access to your platform. This means they can take a lead on opening communications with their target students.
- Make sure the TA has a confidential channel of communication with the student(s) they are working with and access to any modified resources. This will need planning based on a sound knowledge of your platform. In MS Teams you might do this through a private channel, private messaging and/or a separate remote meeting (check what your safeguarding policy has to say about private interactions). In Google Classroom you or the TA might assign particular tasks or resources to particular students – including the link to a separate Meet for student and TA (again, check your safeguarding policy). In Moodle you can create groups within courses and allocate to them different resources – including access to additional remote teaching sessions. A 'group' in this context might be a single student and their TA, just like a Teams channel.

- Even where your TA has particular responsibility for one or two students, where safeguarding is an issue, it is still legitimate to deploy them for short periods to monitor other students. For example, where you have breakout rooms, two of you can keep a better eye than one on the interactions going on there.

Tricky remote teaching scenarios

How difficult you find adapting to remote teaching will depend on a lot of factors – the level and pressure you work at, your ability to pick up new technology, institutional policies and supportiveness – and most important, your students. If you have well-equipped, well-motivated students, it might feel like a seamless transition; you can still achieve great things, but you will face more obstacles. I'd like to finish the chapter by considering a couple of particularly tricky – but far from impossible – scenarios you may face.

Some students are in the physical classroom, others are working remotely

This is likely if you teach the children of keyworkers during a pandemic or if part of your catchment area is on a flood plain and not all students can get in during floods. A particular difficulty here is that you can't focus simultaneously on the physical and remote students. This is awkward when you're explaining something – and really awkward when you have to field multiple questions in both domains. Some tips to manage this include:

- Shift to a more project-based model of delivery. This means that you have more time to spend with individuals. Although in the long term you might find this is not the most efficient delivery model, you may not have to do it for long periods. If the reason for this scenario is predictable, e.g. seasonal floods, you can make sure that you cover topics at this time that lend themselves to more student-centred delivery.
- Unsync physical and remote classes. If you started your remote lesson 15 minutes before or after your physical class, the 'crunch points' where you have multiple queries won't coincide, and you can manage the rest of the lesson. This will work best where either you work part-time or the whole organisation adopts the model, and where you teach relatively long lessons.

Remote teaching with a class that haven't met physically

This can happen if you start remote teaching at the start of the academic year, for example in the event of a pandemic. It is one thing to work remotely with a class you know and who know each other, but quite another to do it 'cold.' You might find that this means that the social needs of the class are not met by remote teaching, leading to general discontent, or it might be that co-operative tasks might be harder. This situation is largely unprecedented, so there are no tried and tested strategies. Nonetheless, the following are worth a try:

- Use lots of problem-based group learning – this encourages productive interaction and can help form a group identity.
- Use lots of assessments and individual tutorials – you need to know the preferences and vulnerabilities of these students, and to know when anyone starts to disengage.

- Use learner-completed, teacher-monitored checklists to check that students are keeping up.
- If possible, issue or recommend a textbook so the students have some source of information and activities other than remote lessons.
- Use the kind of resources and strategies students would use in informal learning – YouTube is the classic example.

Further information

In this chapter I have frequently alluded to the fact that you can achieve more or less the same things using different platforms but that the mechanics of doing so vary by platform. The following links take you to platform-specific instructions.
Google Meet: https://edu.google.com/teacher-center/products/meet/?modal_active=none
MS Teams: https://docs.microsoft.com/en-us/microsoftteams/remote-learning-edu
Zoom: https://zoom.us/education (scroll down for instructions)
For a good list of tools to use synchronously and asynchronously during remote lessons, try this: https://www.teachertoolkit.co.uk/2020/03/15/how-to-teach-online/
For general advice compatible with what I've said in this chapter, try these:
https://www.albert.io/blog/tips-for-teachers-teaching-remotely/
Also, take a look at H. Farmer (2020), 'Six Models for Blended Synchronous and Asynchronous Online Course Delivery,' *Publications and Scholarship*, 2, Sheridan Institutional Repository.

6 Keeping digital education legal, accessible and safe

By the end of this chapter, I hope you will be able to:

- Understand and comply with data protection law
- Understand and comply with copyright law
- Know the requirements of the EU Accessibility Directive and your responsibilities therein
- Make your digital resources accessible to students with a range of abilities and preferences
- Offer basic guidance to students over issues of online safety, including cyberbullying, exploitation and radicalisation
- Be aware of support strategies and referral routes for students at risk of online harm

Digital education and law

Working within the law when teaching digitally can sometimes require a bit of expert knowledge and careful preparation. At the time of writing, three legal frameworks are of particular importance to all organisations and individual teachers: data protection, copyright and accessibility.

Data protection

Data protection law can get complicated, but the principles are straightforward. All personal data is subject to legal protection – this includes names, birth dates, photographs, video, contact details, occupational and financial details, attendance, behaviour records, marks, safeguarding records, records and exam results and qualifications. This applies to you as much as to students, and your Management are obliged to respect your personal data, although in some circumstances such as reference requests, you have to surrender some of your privacy rights. Sensitive personal data such as criminal and medical records have additional protection, so you need to be particularly careful where you hold access to these.

The current legislation comes from the EU's General Data Protection Regulations (2018), absorbed into UK law as the 2018 Data Protection Act (DPA). You might hear about GDPR or DPA – they are essentially the same thing. This requires that all organisations operating within the EU and UK pay close attention to the privacy, extent and uses of the data held on individuals.

DOI: 10.4324/9781003266471-6

Keeping digital education legal, accessible and safe 81

The responsibilities of the organisation

If you are a teacher, most of the collective responsibilities of the school or college will have dealt with at management level. The rest of this section is aimed at teachers. If you are an SLT member, this should have been taken care of; but if in doubt, it is *really* important stuff so I would check with the Information Commissioner's Office (ICO) at https://ico.org.uk/for-organisations/. A member of staff will be nominated as Data Controller. They have responsibility for registering with the Information Commissioner's Office and providing them with up-to-date information on the following:

- What personal data the organisation holds on students and staff
- The purposes for which it holds that data
- Where this data was obtained
- To whom they plan to disclose the data
- Any other countries where they intend to transfer or store the data

As a member of staff who accesses and works with student data, you are classified as a data processor, and you also have some responsibility for keeping data secure.

Digital learning platforms

As long as you are using a digital platform set up by your school or college, you as a teacher should be fairly safe as regards data protection. Using external applications can be much more problematic, however. Bear in mind the following:

- If you share student data with an external site or encourage them to do so, and the site is hacked or behaves irresponsibly, you – in the role of data processor – and/or your school or college may be held liable. So, make sure your Data Controller has approved any sites to which your students sign up and be prepared to pass the buck back to them if anything goes wrong. If in any doubt, talk to your Data Controller. They may seem overly cautious, but the consequences of getting this wrong can be serious, so don't be tempted to give them the slip. Remember that the UK age of data consent is 13. This means that a young person must be at least 13 to consent to having their data processed. This is why social media companies will not knowingly deal with under-13s. If you teach under-13s, it becomes even more critical that you do not encourage them to sign up for accounts with unapproved external educational providers.
- Student data must generally be held on servers within the UK or EU. American companies can still hold personal data from EU citizens but generally only on servers located in the EU. So large American companies like Google, Microsoft and Nearpod are okay, but if you are unsure about a site, check that they have European servers. A notice on a company's homepage stating that it meets GDPR rules does *not* necessarily indicate that it meets them to a standard acceptable to the Information Commissioner, so always search independent reviews before signing up.
- Your use of synchronous remote teaching tools like MS Teams and Google Meet will be covered by terms of your school or college account, and data can be kept secure

between users. Unless your school or college has an institutional account, be very careful about using other tools. The moment you input a learner's name and email to invite them to an external site, you risk being in breach of GDPR. There are ongoing arguments as to whether some sites that claim to be GDPR-compliant really are.

- This is one place where you can easily go wrong even if working on an organisational account: Holding personally identifiable data requires specific and current permissions. So, any surveys or forms that collect names or emails, or any recordings of student faces or voices, require voluntary agreement to a GDPR statement and a rationale for storing that data. Recording audio or video of students also collects identifiable information, so again, this should have a suitable GDPR statement and be voluntary. Prior catchall consent and presumed consent are not sufficient, so make sure that all surveys and assignments that collect personal data include a GDPR statement, and gain permission.

Personal devices and accounts

If you have a school or college device, it should be secure – chances are it has an encrypted hard drive and you need two-factor authentication to access content. Organisational data sticks – unlike your own – are also likely to be encrypted. Unless you are particularly tech-savvy, chances are that your personal devices are much less secure than work ones. This is why an increasing number of schools and colleges now ban or discourage the use of data sticks and prefer or mandate the use of work laptops and phones. Institutional policies like not storing important passwords in browsers are a pain in the proverbial, but they do significantly reduce the likelihood of a data breach.

Accessing data that you are entitled to access on a personal machine is not illegal or in itself a data breach. However, if your devices are less secure, then it does make a data breach more likely. Your personal device may log on to an unsecured or inadequately secured network, be lost or stolen or, particularly in the case of Android devices, have insecure third-party apps that can be hacked to gain access to data from the phone or tablet. If a breach occurs and your choice of personal hardware is a contributing factor, you may be considered to be negligent and subject to disciplinary processes. I don't normally take sides in the Apple wars, but note that Apple devices are widely regarded as significantly more secure than most of the hardware than run Windows or Android.

Be particularly aware of the importance of not using personal remote teaching apps for teaching. It is easy to inadvertently share emails between classmates (technically a data breach), and students will assume that granting permission to be recorded means on the school or college space, not that of their teacher. So don't record lessons on a personal Zoom account. Most seriously, if something really inappropriate is shared during a recorded session, you personally, as opposed to the school, will find yourself in possession of it.

Private online tutoring

If you are a private tutor and hold personal data on your students (which you will – you can't achieve much without their name and email address), you are subject to the same regulations as a school. You need to register with the ICO and make the same declarations as a school. You are then effectively a Data Controller and as such you need to have a good knowledge of the regulations. You need proper consent from your students for the data you collect, as well as a straightforward way for them to report a suspected breach and request access to or deletion of the personal data that you hold on them. And remember the age of data consent. You will need parental permission and give parental rights to access and deletion if the tutee is under 13. I would suggest it is still best practice if the tutee is aged 13–16.

Your tutoring account should have a reasonable level of security. I recommend having a Google Workspace account for tutoring. This gives you fully featured Google Meet, Google Classroom and Gmail as well as standard business-level security including two-factor authentication for less than £10 a month. You don't need to give your students a corporate email – that would just add to the cost. If you set up your own Moodle for tutoring, you can access a set of instructions and tools from Moodle HQ to make it GDPR-compliant – it isn't compliant straight out of the box.

All the same provisos about hardware security apply if you tutor privately – more so, really, as you alone are responsible. Make sure data sticks are encrypted (or not used), that the desktop or laptop from which you work has an encrypted hard drive and that you store passwords that would allow access to student data securely – e.g. in an encrypted spreadsheet, not in the browser.

Print-outs

Data protection law applies as much to printed material as it does to digital. You should therefore treat printed material containing personal data with the same level of seriousness. When printing, make sure the machine is working, and don't leave it with a data document in the print queue; if it prints out after you leave, and students see it, that is a data breach. This is why schools and colleges are now widely using managed printing solutions – if you have that option, take it. Documents should always be stored in a locked cabinet.

Accessibility

In digital education, accessibility refers to the ease with which students and staff with a range of disabilities, cognitive abilities and preferences can make full use of technology. Physical disabilities might, for example, prevent people from using keyboards and/or mice. Sensory impairments might make it difficult to use a standard screen or listen to a conversation. Cognitive impairments might impact on the ability to make sense of complex instructions or focus on a 'busy' screen. In practice, accessibility needs are quite idiosyncratic, and there is no substitute to working with individuals to see what works for them.

Legal obligations

Exactly what you *have* to do in law around accessibility depends on what sector you work in. However, there is a strong ethical case for all teachers to make reasonable efforts to ensure that their digital content is accessible. Since 2020, the EU Accessibility Directive has required that all public sector and public-funded websites in the United Kingdom comply to the following standards:

- Content should be perceivable to any user, including those with disabilities
- Activities should be operable by any user
- Content should be as understandable as possible
- Content and activities should work on any kind of device and operating system

UK Schools and 6th-form colleges are exempt from the EU directive; however, FE colleges, universities and private and charitable training providers who access public funding are required to adhere to them. If you are in an FE college or private training company, you may be able to claim that implementing some requirements would be an unreasonable burden or are beyond your control, as you are linking to externally provided content over which you have no editorial control. However, you must still be seen to be making reasonable efforts to comply with the regulations, including having an institutional accessibility policy and undertaking accessibility audits.

Carrying out an audit

Technically, accessibility auditing has been a legal requirement since 2020, but the government treated this sensitively as it coincided with additional burdens on digital educators during the pandemic. Now, however, it should be taken seriously. Small organisations such as private training companies are permitted to carry out a basic accessibility audit. A full guide to conducting a basic accessibility audit can be found on the UK government website (https://www.gov.uk/government/publications/doing-a-basic-accessibility-check-if-you-cant-do-a-detailed-one/doing-a-basic-accessibility-check-if-you-cant-do-a-detailed-one), but, briefly, the following are the things you as a teacher should try to ensure:

- Where possible, information should ideally be on a web page rather than a document, because HTML files are more accessible. However, there is the ability when conducting an accessibility audit to claim that document handouts, worksheets and other forms are essential for your business.
- Text (whether on a web page or document) should have proper headings, not simply emboldened or changed in size. This allows assistive technology like screen readers to make sense of a page. Text size should be changeable without affecting the use of the page; this is important for visually impaired people.
- Pages (web and document) should have clear, descriptive titles so that a reader who cannot visually scan whole pages can decide whether to proceed and read them. Subtitles should be logically nested (e.g. H1, H2, H3, H3, H3, H2, H3, H3), so that readers using a screen reader can navigate around a page.
- Web pages should work with styles disabled, so that users who get overwhelmed by too much visual information can work with a simplified page.
- Images should have an alt text description so that a visually impaired reader can extract all the information provided on a page.

- Video and audio should have transcripts so that people who cannot or choose not to make use of video can still extract all the necessary information from a page containing video.
- Live video, e.g. in remote lessons, should have the option of showing captions for the benefit of auditory-impaired students.
- Forms and other interactives should have submit buttons clearly labelled so that anyone can use them regardless of visual acuity.
- There is a minimum contrast between text and background, depending on text size, so that mild to moderately visually impaired people are likely to be able to see the page. You can check this here: https://webaim.org/resources/contrastchecker/.
- Sentences should be short and unambiguous, with only well-known abbreviations.
- Web pages work on any browser on any device. This means they cannot rely on outdated technology like Flash and Java.

This is not a comprehensive list, and no amount of preparation is a substitute for working individually with students to ensure that their needs are met. However, it gives a flavour of the kind of things you should look at. A basic accessibility checklist is provided in the Appendix.

Typically, schools and colleges are not small organisations and will need to carry out a full audit. This should be carried out by a properly qualified in-house accessibility expert or more usually a consultant. The government recommends a set fee of £1300 for this. If you put this out to tender and receive only offers substantially more expensive than this, you may be able to claim that carrying out a full audit is a disproportionate burden and carry out a basic audit in house.

Browser accessibility

Your browser will have some basic accessibility tools built in. For example, you can zoom in and out of a page to make it easier to read. You can enhance your browser's capabilities considerably using the AT Bar (www.atbar.org). This can live in your browser as an extension or in the page code of websites including some learning platforms. When activated, the AT Bar offers the following:

- Increase font size without zooming into a page
- Change the page font to one of your choice
- Spellcheck your answers to form fields and quiz questions
- Look up words in an online dictionary
- Read highlighted text aloud
- Use predictive text
- Change page styles, including switching to high- and low-contrast versions
- Place coloured overlays in front of web pages

If you use Moodle, the AT Bar is one of the tools that can be opened in an accessibility block.

Making documents and presentations accessible

The issues outlined here apply equally to any content you make available on your digital learning platform. As a teacher, this is more important, really – you can't be held personally responsible for breaches on a school learning platform, but you can be for your own handouts, worksheets and presentations. This means headings must use H tags – it is technically illegal to post handouts and presentations in which headings are simply emboldened and/or enlarged text. Images must have alt text. You can use technical terms in documents and presentations, but you still need to keep sentences short and clear, with a minimum of non-technical long words. Presentations must use sufficiently large text and high text-background contrast ratio – if you are preparing slides on a small screen for projection, always allow a higher contrast than you need on the small screen.

If you weren't aware of the Accessibility Directive, you might be shocked at the word 'illegal.' So far, this has not been aggressively enforced, but it is there, and forewarned is forearmed. For full guidance on making documents and presentations accessible see Microsoft's site: https://support.microsoft.com/en-us/office/make-your-content-accessible-to-everyone-ecab0fcf-d143-4fe8-a2ff-6cd596bddc6d?ui=en-us&rs=en-us&ad=us.

Making live remote teaching accessible

Some videoconferencing apps are inherently more accessible than others, and if you are choosing an app for students with particular needs, it is well worth considering which you choose. Like all apps, remote teaching tools need to be keyboard-operable, and they have additional specific requirements:

- Closed captions: live subtitles for what is being said.
- Transcript: A text file is generated after a remote lesson.
- Chat/instant messaging: This allows a teacher – or, better still, a TA – to clarify points and reassure students.

The good news is that the big four – Zoom, Meet, Teams and BigBlueButton – have all these features. However, if you have low visual acuity, you will be lucky to find the meeting button in Teams or the settings in Zoom. Although these apps have a good range of accessibility features, this capability has not as yet been matched in the design of the interface. At the time of writing, I therefore recommend Meet as the tool of choice for remote teaching, where accessibility is a priority.

Copyright

Probably the most common legal breaches committed by teachers are in respect of copyright. Copyright law is currently in transition, with the EU having approved a set of new rules that are set to make life quite uncomfortable for teachers after 2021. However (at the time of writing), it is not clear what aspects of the directive may make their way into UK law or how vigorously they will be policed. This section is therefore necessarily brief, but I will offer some thoughts on common issues arising.

Images

You will undoubtedly use pictures in teaching materials that have been obtained online. There is some confusion around about what you are allowed to use and what is off limits. Many photobanks offer royalty-free images, but note that *royalty*-free is not the same as *copyright*-free. Royalty-free simply means that a fee is not payable per use; sites can still require a flat fee for their use. A smaller number of photobanks offer genuinely copyright-free images, and that's what you are after. These include the following:

- Pixabay (htttps://www.pixabay.com)
- Unsplash (https://www.unsplash.com)
- StockSnap (https://stocksnap.io)
- Pexels (https://pexels.com)
- Wikimedia Commons (https://commons.wikimedia.org/wiki/Main_Page)

Do check the licencing details on each site. Some images are free to use in the financial sense but require a visible attribution on your resource.

Two other common sources of images are Flickr and Google Images. There is nothing dodgy about Flickr, but note that there are eight types of licence in use on the site, and that not all users will have understood them when posting. If you are using Flickr, ensure that you understand these variations in permissions. Google images can be filtered for Creative Commons licences. Although all of these should be legal for educational purposes, check whether attribution is required.

Video

Under legacy copyright law you are responsible for copyright breaches if you upload video files to your site, but not if you link to a video-sharing site like YouTube. The responsibility lies with the host. However, the new EU legislation includes a 'link tax,' meaning that schools and colleges will either have to obtain permission from the copyright holder to link to a video or to be prepared to be charged. This may not end up being implemented or enforced in UK law, but it's one to keep an eye on.

Text

Teachers currently have an exemption for the use of copyright material for teaching purposes. So, you can post extracts from copyright-restricted textbooks and articles provided you are working on a secure password-protected education platform. If you have a learning platform that permits public access, you will be much more limited in what you can share on those public pages. As for video, keep a close eye out for future changes in the law.

E-safety

Most digital learning does not directly expose students to online risk; however, risk is present whenever anyone goes online. Schools, colleges and anyone working with young or otherwise vulnerable people have moral and legal obligations to mitigate this risk. To thoroughly review every potential online risk and a good range of strategies for dealing with them would take a longer book than this. What I can do in the space available is to equip you with a basic understanding of what online risks exist, what your school or college should be doing and what you can do as an individual to support students.

> **Top tech tip**: This section is necessarily sensitive and upsetting, involving mention of suicide, sexual abuse and terrorism. I have tried to put things in a matter-of-fact way for the sake of clarity, but this will not stop you experiencing some strong reactions. That's normal and healthy, and it does *not* mean you aren't tough enough for safeguarding work, just that you are human.

A typology of online risks

There are various ways of classifying online risk, so don't take this as definitive, but I've found it helpful to start with the OECD's 2021 typology.

- Content risks: hateful content, harmful content, illegal content and disinformation.
- Conduct risks: hateful behaviour, harmful behaviour, illegal behaviour and user-generated problem behaviour.
- Contact risks: hateful encounters, harmful encounters, illegal encounters and other problematic encounters.
- Consumer risks: marketing risks, commercial profiling risks, financial risks and security risks.

Privacy risks and risks to health and well-being cut across these four categories.

Hateful content can take the form of words but also memes and songs. Anonymity and distance make it easier to insult online, and online discourse frequently involves insulting references to gender, race, sexuality and other attributes. According to Ofcom (2020), half of 12- to 15-year-olds had witnessed online hate. Content can have harmful effects, particularly if it is age inappropriate. Thus, violent and sexually explicit content – and particularly sexually violent content – can traumatise children and young people. Much of the most shocking and upsetting material is also illegal, including, for example, child sexual abuse and terrorism. More recently, the emphasis in understanding content risks has turned to disinformation. It is critical – though sometimes extremely difficult – to equip students to recognise fake news and propaganda. Combined disinformation and shocking images are present when attempts are made to radicalise.

Risky behaviours to which children are exposed include discriminatory abuse, but can be bespoke as well as based on demographics – the key thing is the intention to cause distress. Where this is sustained over time, it constitutes cyberbullying. Critically, risky conduct includes that initiated by students. This can include cyberbullying – which is often, though not necessarily, carried out by students unaware of the effects of their actions.

Cyberbullying

Surveys consistently show that a significant minority of secondary-age children (15-20%) experience one or more nasty behaviours that we might call 'cyberbullying,' although interestingly, around half of these do not themselves think of it as bullying. Common nasty online behaviour includes:

- Name calling
- Sending abusive messages, either directly through messaging apps or on online platforms, games and chatrooms
- Deliberate exclusion from groups
- Spreading rumours via social media
- Threats
- Deliberate exposure to hate material

This makes cyberbullying rather less common than face-to-face bullying. There is no major difference in the number of male and female victims; however, young people with chronic physical and, in particular, mental health conditions are at elevated risk. The majority of incidents are perpetrated by someone at the same school.

The impact of cyberbullying on well-being is significant, with the majority of victims reporting that they are affected or seriously affected. Common effects include depression and anxiety, underachievement in education, reduced popularity status and a smaller number of friends. A meta-analysis of studies by John et al (2018) showed that victims of cyberbullying were two to three times as likely as others to self-harm and attempt suicide. Because cyberbullying can be carried out anonymously, and because victims can be reached at any time through electronic devices, it is particularly harmful and difficult to deal with.

What schools/colleges can do

The NSPCC and the Anna Freud Centre recommend the following:

- A pastoral approach that celebrates diversity and emphasises co-operation, empathy, tolerance, relationship building and assertiveness to resist pressure
- A whole-school approach where all staff and parents are aware of policies and staff are confident to recognise and tackle cases. This means training for staff and students
- An effective bullying policy that includes a detailed and up-to-date understanding of cyberbullying, clear procedures for anyone experiencing and witnessing bullying, and clear and consistent responses to incidents

What you can do

- Make it clear that bullying is a personal priority for you, and that you *will* intervene
- Know who your DSL/DSO (Designated Safeguarding Lead/Deputy Safeguarding Lead/Designated Safeguarding Officer) is and liaise with them over any suspicions

- Always respond to observations or disclosures and involve the DSL/DSO
- Be as non-judgmental as possible, even if you are dealing with a bully – they are not two-dimensional Bond villains and will have a backstory you are not privy to that affects their actions
- Listen to disclosures and, as much as possible, avoid asking leading questions
- Record disclosures immediately, and make sure victims screen-shot evidence

NANNIs (sexting)

Some degree of content risk is inevitable wherever people interact online. Where your own students interact with one another, there is always a simultaneous opportunity for enhanced learning and a risk of compromised safety. Contact becomes a risk whenever it exposes students to hate, is intended to harm them, is illegal or is exploitative in nature – of course these categories are not mutually exclusive. In some cases, people actively engage in behaviour potentially harmful to themselves.

The classic example is the sharing of NANNIs – nude or nearly nude images – what is often called sexting. It is easy to be judgmental about this kind of sharing; however, it is very much a normal part of contemporary relationship behaviour – and not just for young people. The average age of someone sexting in the context of a romantic relationship is probably somewhere in the 50s. This statistic gives us a powerful tool to make sexting uncool – no teenager wants to emulate the trends of their parents' generation.

And it *is* important to discourage sexting in under-18s. This is not just an old dude being judgy – an under-18 who shares an explicit image of themselves or others is technically guilty of producing and distributing child pornography and may end up criminalised. It may also prove difficult for a teenager to keep control over images once they have been shared, and the idea that an image shared with a partner may eventually end up being traded amongst sex offenders is naturally extremely distressing for a young person, sometimes even ending in suicide. A related problem is revenge porn, the deliberate sharing of explicit material, generally by an ex, with the aim of causing distress. By sexting, a student leaves themselves vulnerable to a later revenge porn incident.

What schools/colleges can do

- Make reference to sexting or NANNIs in their Child Protection Policy.
- Share this policy in an age-appropriate way with students.
- Implement a procedure involving meeting between the DSL, staff involved and students involved in order to establish facts and risks.
- Inform parents unless doing so might put the child or young person at further risk.
- Where there is concern for the child or young person's safety or well-being, a police referral will need to be made. Unless there are complicating factors (e.g. a big age difference between 'sexter' and 'sextee'), this is unlikely to lead to the child or young person being criminalised (this is known as Outcome 21).

What you can do

- Do not offer confidentiality – you *will* have to bring this to the DSL.
- Be non-judgmental – sexting is normal sexual behaviour for many people.
- Don't look at the images. This might sound obvious, but actually it is quite common for a young person disclosing the events to hand you a device to illustrate what they are saying. Looking, however, will be traumatic for both of you.
- Reassure the child or young person that they are *unlikely* to end up criminalised but don't make a promise you can't keep.
- As with all safeguarding disclosures, listen, avoid leading questions and keep notes.
- Offer to sit in on the police interview if one takes place.

Sexual exploitation

We need to recognise that young people integrate the online environment into every aspect of their lives, so we should not be surprised when this extends to romantic and sexual aspects. However, this should not be confused with deliberate sexual exploitation. Ten years ago, most grooming was geared towards meeting in the physical world whereupon abuse would be enacted. However, although this still happens, there has been a growth in grooming culminating in attempts to engage a victim in online sexual activity. This is typically recorded and may be followed up by sextortion – once an abuser has explicit images and/or video of a victim, they may use this to blackmail them to participate in further activity and/or to pay money.

It is easy to assume that students must be doing something dubious online to leave themselves vulnerable to grooming by sex offenders. However, this is absolutely not the case. Sex offenders often have an innocent-appearing online persona with which to infiltrate communities where vulnerable people might be found. Exploitation usually begins with befriending and only gradually escalates to abuse. Sites where grooming takes place range from gaming sites and their accompanying social media (e.g. Discord), through more generic social media (e.g. Snapchat), to bereavement and chronic illness support sites, where people can be found at their most vulnerable. This is *not* an argument against the use of any of those apps or sites, but young people should be made aware of the risks before using them.

Financial exploitation

Online contacts may also exploit students financially in a number of ways:

- *Scamming*: We would be wrong to assume that financial scams are aimed exclusively at older, wealthier people. Students are extensively targeted by scammers and tricked into transferring money.
- *Extortion*: Old-fashioned demanding money with menaces may occur online as well as face-to-face. Students are forced to transfer money to others' accounts in a modern reworking of traditional dinner money theft.

- *Identity theft*: Children and young people are fifty times as likely to have their identity stolen as opposed to an adult. It is easier to steal their identities because there are no complex financial records to duplicate, just a blank state.
- *Muling*: This is a form of money laundering in which money is transferred to a legitimate bank account and either withdrawn and passed on as cash or transferred out to another account. Students might be intimidated, misled or paid to carry this out, often without their realising that money laundering is a serious criminal offence – and one for which there is a permanent record of their participation.
- *Doxing*: Stealing and/or sharing personal information online. This is not always with the aim of financial exploitation – it can be a prank or part of a cyberbullying campaign. However, often the leaked details are sufficient to allow criminals to create new bank accounts in the name of the victim.
- *Teen financial abuse*: the term 'financial abuse' has a more specific meaning than how it sounds – it means to control someone's ability to acquire, keep or spend money within the context of a romantic or family relationship. Abusive partners of students might demand they pay for dates or transfer money to them, or they might simply demand that they save money to spend on things that benefit the abuser e.g. holidays together. Students age 18+ might even be made responsible for payments on a credit card in their partner's name. Parents can also be responsible for financial abuse.

What schools/colleges can do

- Make reference to exploitation in their Child Protection Policy
- Make sure staff have suitable training
- Provide age-appropriate training on exploitation in the pastoral programme
- Inform parents and the police as appropriate

What you can do

- Again, do not offer confidentiality – you will need to bring this to the DSL
- Be non-judgmental and reassure victims of exploitation that they are just that – victims
- As with sexting, don't look at any images, but encourage the victim to keep evidence
- As with all safeguarding disclosures, listen, avoid leading questions and keep notes
- Offer to sit in on the police interview if one takes place

> **Top tech tip:** It can be really helpful for an anxious student to have a trusted teacher or TA present in a police interview. You don't have to worry, though; in my experience these interviews are always carried out sensitively by highly trained officers and leave students feeling better about the situation.

Radicalisation

Radicalisation is the process through which a person becomes a supporter, and perhaps an active participant in, extremist ideologies. Radicalisation is harmful in itself, as it is likely to leave an individual feeling angry and disconnected from those around them, not to mention distracted from their education. However, the reason radicalisation has such a high profile as a potential harm has more to do with the links between extremist ideology and terrorism.

So, what is an extremist ideology? The UK government's counter-extremism strategy (2015) says that:

> Extremism is the vocal or active opposition to our fundamental values, including democracy, the rule of law, individual liberty, and respect and tolerance for different faiths and beliefs. We also regard calls for the death of members of our armed forces as extremist.

In practice, the extremist ideologies you are most likely to come across depend on where you live, but are likely to include the Far Right and Islamism.

The UK government's Prevent Strategy was launched in 2011, with four broad aims: to define fundamental British values and place a clear boundary between beliefs that are compatible and those that are incompatible with them; to support vulnerable people at risk of falling into terrorism; to work with organisations, including schools and colleges, where people can be radicalised; and to make technology use safe from hateful content and contact.

> **Top tech tip**: The Prevent programme is controversial in some circles, because initially the focus was very much on the Muslim community. However, a lot has been learned in the last decade, and the Prevent of the 2020s is quite different. I really urge all those who were concerned or offended (as I was) by the early approach to engage actively and positively with the current Prevent Strategy, which is now much more sophisticated and non-discriminatory.

What schools/colleges can do

Since 2015 schools and colleges have a statutory duty to support Prevent, in particular to:

- Risk-assess children and young people who may be vulnerable to becoming radicalised
- Refer those at particular risk e.g. those who reveal a personal extremist ideology to Channel, the UK government's early intervention programme
- Work with the Local Safeguarding Children Board, who are responsible at local level for implementing Prevent
- Engage meaningfully with parents and the local community so that they understand what Prevent is for
- Train staff – at a minimum, the DSL should provide training, and this can be usefully supplemented by a WRAP-accredited trainer (WRAP = Workshop for Raising Awareness of Prevent)

What you can do

- Encourage open and respectful debate about controversial topics as they come up in class, challenging extreme ideas in a friendly, respectful way, *aiming to trump the arguments* without humiliating the student

- Refer disclosures or expressions of extremist ideology to the DSL
- Keep in mind that students undergoing radicalisation are victims of a particular form of exploitation, just as much as if they were being exploited sexually or financially
- As with all safeguarding disclosures, listen, avoid leading questions and keep notes
- Offer to sit in on the DSL/Channel interview if one takes place

Further information

The Data Protection Act (2018) is available online at https://www.legislation.gov.uk/ukpga/2018/12/part/2. For the most complete and up-to-date information about data protection, try the Information Commissioner's Office at https://ico.org.uk/your-data-matters/schools/

To keep up to date with policy as regards web accessibility, keep an eye on the UK government website: https://www.gov.uk/guidance/accessibility-requirements-for-public-sector-websites-and-apps. The amazing JISC also publish guidance here: https://www.jisc.ac.uk/accessibility. You can read guidance on the use of free online accessibility checkers here – https://usabilitygeek.com/10-free-web-based-web-site-accessibility-evaluation-tools/ – but do read their warning before using them. Remember that copyright law may change imminently; for now, universities provide some good advice to staff, so you could do worse than to look at this – especially if it changes! You could start with this practical guide from York University: https://subjectguides.york.ac.uk/copyright/teaching#:~:text=Teachers%20and%20students%20are%20able,tickets%2C%20or%20recording%20the%20performance

There are a great many sites aiming to support e-safety. For cyberbullying try the NSPCC at https://www.nspcc.org.uk/what-is-child-abuse/types-of-abuse/bullying-and-cyberbullying/. The National Bullying Helpline also provide excellent advice for victims at https://www.nationalbullyinghelpline.co.uk/cyberbullying.html. For resources to help you help young people with online relationships including sexting, try https://www.thinkuknow.co.uk/professionals/resources/11-18s-toolkit/ and https://saferinternet.org.uk/guide-and-resource/sexting-resources. To help combat online sexual exploitation, CEOP publish a newsletter here: https://www.thinkuknow.co.uk/professionals/resources/editable-newsletter-for-parents-and-carers-secondary/. You can also get advice here: https://saferinternet.org.uk/online-issue/coerced-online-child-sexualabuse. There is less online advice on financial exploitation of young people than you might imagine, but you could start with this from The Money Pages: https://www.themoneypages.com/saving-banking/young-people-increased-risk-financial-crime/

You can read the Prevent Strategy in full here: https://assets.publishing.service.gov.uk/government/uploads/system/uploads/attachment_data/file/97976/prevent-strategy-review.pdf. Guidance for schools can be found here: https://www.gov.uk/government/publications/prevent-duty-guidance. Resources for students can be found at https://educateagainsthate.com/teachers/ and https://preventforfeandtraining.org.uk/home/leaders-and-managers/useful-resources/

The Ofcom (2020) *Online nation* report is available at https://www.ofcom.org.uk/__data/assets/pdf_file/0027/196407/online-nation-2020-report.pdf. Also see HM Government (2015), *Counter-extremism strategy*, London, Counter-extremism Directorate; and John et al (2018), Self-harm, suicidal behaviours, and cyberbullying in children and young people: Systematic review. *Journal of Medical Internet Research*, 20(4), p. e9044.

7 Digital leadership and change

By the end of this chapter, I hope you will be able to:

- Be clear about the range of tasks and skills involved in digital leadership and change
- Map your organisational digital preferences and capabilities
- Establish a digital development plan, from vision to individual actions
- Classify potential changes according to the SAMR model and understand the different planning decisions deriving from each classification
- Use co-design principles to plan changes in the use of education technology
- Understand the importance of implementing and anchoring change, evaluating the impact of technological change and giving thought to decommissioning

This chapter is particularly for those with a stake in planning, managing and contributing to digital change in a school or college – or, of course, those who aspire to such a role. There is no one-size-fits-all, end-to-end solution here, but I can provide you with some strategies and tools to aid your thinking and planning.

Digital leadership

Traditionally, management structures have not included senior roles devoted to e-learning or educational technology, and if you are lucky enough to have SLT members with detailed understanding of digital education, you are still more the exception than the rule. In the absence of such a perfectly placed expert, it is probably worth investing in one or more staff members to acquire the necessary expertise.

Digital learning CPD

Well-respected sources of training include the following:

- The Association for Learning Technology (ALT) provides three levels of accreditation, assessed by portfolio and supported by peer mentors. The cost is trivial and the timing flexible, although all but the initial associate level require a reasonable body of digital education experience to draw on. The two higher levels constitute professional accreditation as a Learning Technologist, however, you may find that if you or your designed

staff member(s) are looking to bring a digital element to more generic management roles, the associate level may be adequate for your needs.
- JISC provide a Digital Leaders Programme. This is a short but very intensive programme, taking place over four taught days plus assignments. It can be completed remotely (eight half-day sessions over a month) or in person (two two-day residentials). The focus is on understanding the school or college through a digital lens and understanding and planning organisational change. This carries a more substantial cost, particularly for schools, who are not eligible for JISC membership. But until you have someone undertake a course like this, it is hard to appreciate how much there is to know, and how much you simply didn't know, about digital planning and change.

A knowledgeable, reliable and open-minded consultant can also be extremely helpful, but don't confuse consultancy with sales. A digital learning consultant should start from an analysis of your current state of digital development and your organisational needs rather than simply advocate for a particular set of pre-selected tools.

The scope of digital leadership skills

Whether you contract in expertise or develop yourself and/or your own staff, and whether you distribute responsibilities between several people or concentrate elements of digital expertise and leadership in one role, it is important to understand the range of attributes your digital leader(s) will need.

- *Tech savvy*: The digital leader needs to have, or the willingness to rapidly develop a good awareness of, a range of digital ed apps and detailed knowledge of a smaller number. Generic IT expertise and generic management expertise are ultimately not sufficient – digital learning is a field all of its own.
- *Pedagogy savvy*: It's not ultimately about what technology you use, but how you use it. This requires a good understanding of learning.
- *Inspirational*: The digital leader will be responsible for effecting substantial changes in the way teachers go about their work. Assuming you prefer co-operation to blind obedience, this means winning hearts and minds. The digital leader needs to be able to persuade and inspire users across a wide spectrum of experience and attitudes
- *Innovative*: A good digital leader needs to be able to develop novel solutions by using technology in new ways in response to changing needs and scenarios. They don't need to be a developer, but they do need to be able to think outside the box about how to use applications.
- *Empathic*: Charisma and innovation are important but need to be offset by empathy. Teachers suffer from initiative overload and have good reasons to be cautious about change. A degree of willingness to listen to their concerns and work with individuals to manage initial workload and show the personal benefits of tech change will go a long way.
- *Open-minded*: Just as the ability to inspire needs to be balanced with willingness to listen, so expertise in particular technologies and ways of using it needs to be balanced

with openness to considering different solutions and perspectives. What has been shown to work in one setting may well work in another, but that is not to say that it is the only or best solution for that context.

Understanding your organisation

We work in contexts where change is often a response to expectations from on high, and, in the face of top-down initiatives, it is common to feel you lack options. However, once we are aware of this tendency, we have more freedom to choose how to respond. And of course, we do sometimes initiate our own plans or make informed decisions to stick with our current systems and procedures. Whatever the circumstances, it is *always* desirable to begin a process of decision-making with a good understanding of your starting point. In the case of digital learning, this means your current digital environment and capabilities, the expectations of your students and the experience and opinions of your staff.

Mapping your current tech use

A good start to any wide-ranging programme of change – or, indeed, to justify *not* changing – is to brainstorm all the apps you currently use in the organisation. Don't assume you know these; you'll need to involve a good range of people in this exercise to identify a range of applications. Some people have found it helpful to plot each application on two dimensions; organisational vs individual creative control, and transmission vs interactive models of delivery. Typically, you will find that the applications most valued by teachers tend to fall either in the top or right halves. See Figure 7.1 for an example – note that this is just an example, and that you really need to look at this in your own school or college. Your staff might use different apps or use them in imaginative ways that vary substantially from how they are represented here.

Recall the principles of learning and psychological theories outlined in Chapter 1. In line with self-determination theory, teachers tend to be more motivated to use applications under their creative control – and this is doubly true when they can actually own their account (which is actually okay, as long as they do not create student accounts or otherwise facilitate sharing of identifiable student data). This explains why so many teachers love Padlet and Trello, even though their functionality is limited. This preference for functionally basic applications outside organisational control can be a source of huge frustration for both Learning Technologists and managers, but we should probably accept it to some degree and make our policies accordingly flexible.

Students are probably more concerned with interactivity than their teacher's creative control. Transmission-oriented applications – those which simply display information in some form – are hard to reconcile with the principles of active and interactive learning. Perhaps more importantly, they tend to be at odds with the controllable prosumer ethos of most of the applications we encounter outside formal education.

One more thing to consider when considering the dimensions of control and interactivity is affordances (see the 'Affordances' section of Chapter 1, p. 7). Some apps can be used in very different ways; VLE technology *affords* high levels of transmission and low levels of

Digital leadership and change   99

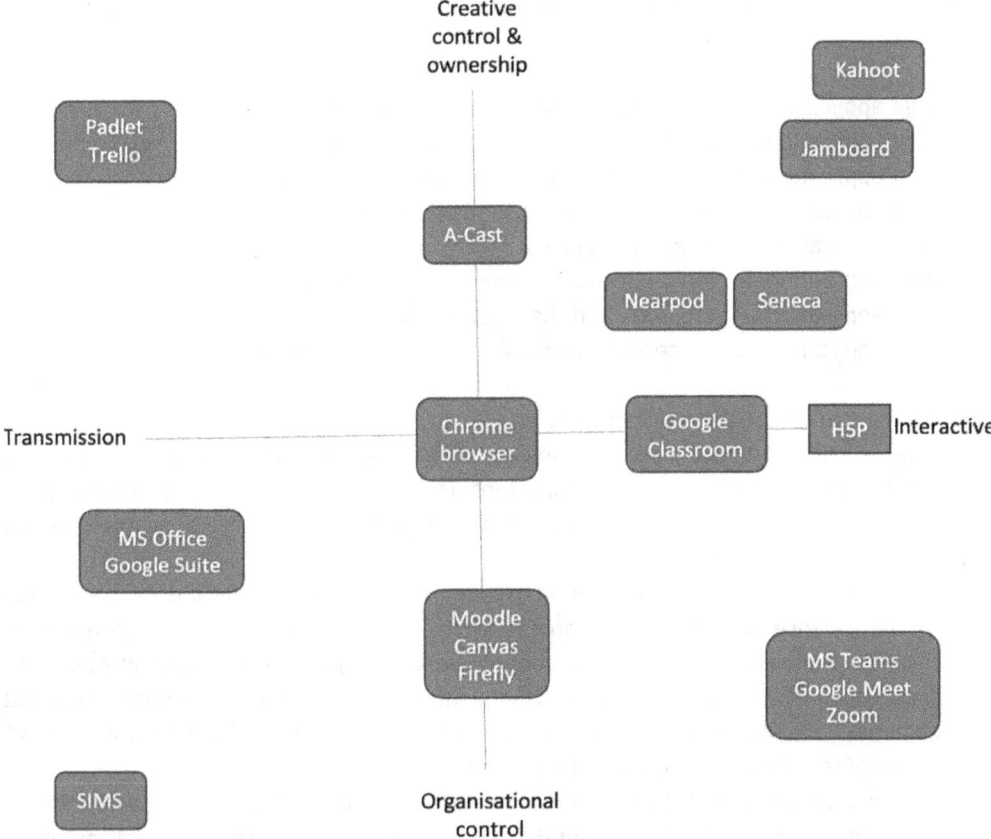

Figure 7.1 An example of applications used by a school plotted on dimensions of interactivity and control.

creative control. However, affordances are a product of appearance rather than of functionality. VLEs like Canvas and Moodle *look like* corporate repositories for curating static resources like documents and presentations. Of course, this isn't the only or best way to use a VLE, but they do tend to look like that's what they are for. So, unless you have a strategy for effective use, VLEs tend to generate low staff and student ratings for ownership and interactivity. This reveals a VLE-development and staff training need, and it is not a reason to move away from your VLE.

Mapping staff and student preferences

This is *much* trickier than you might think, and many digital change programmes falter or go off track at this point. The first uncomfortable task is to admit (in private, anyway) that staff will *not* all be exclusively, enthusiastically or effectively using all the tools mentioned in your policies, and even where they are, there is likely to be a gulf between management, teacher and student perceptions of them. So, if you really want to know your teacher and student capabilities and preferences, forget your policies and go to your users.

Second, you need to define what you actually want to know. These are some of the questions you might be considering:

- What applications do teachers use most often on a day-to-day basis?
- What applications do teachers consider the most important?
- What applications do teachers find to be the most user-friendly?
- What applications do teachers value most as pedagogically useful?
- What applications do students use most often on a day-to-day basis?
- What applications do students consider the most important?
- What applications do students find the most user-friendly?
- What applications do students value most as pedagogically useful?

It is easy to conflate these questions, leading to dubious conclusions. If you really want to know what applications have a profound impact on engagement and learning, don't ask what folks use most often or consider most important. That kind of question is likely to lead to an overemphasis on basics like online registers and email, which are clearly important but don't impact directly on learning.

There is also a balance to be maintained between what is user-friendly and what is impactful, but this balance will not be the same in every situation. Where your emphasis is on stretching the most able and/or you are confident about engagement, your emphasis might be more on applications with high impact. On the other hand, in environments where student engagement is a challenge, user-friendly applications should probably have a higher status – modest benefits to learning are better than none.

Finally, don't assume that teachers know what students like or that students know what's good for them. Egg-sucking, I'm sure, but if you want to know what managers think, ask managers. If you want to know what teachers think, ask teachers, and if you want to know what students think, ask students. The views of all may be important, but they are *not* the same thing and shouldn't be muddled up. Here is a simple example. As a manager, you are probably most used to the Office 365 environment. You cannot assume from your experiences that teachers or students see Office 365 the same way – chances are that most students and younger teachers actually prefer Google technology.

At this stage in the process, you are interested in gathering qualitative data, so it's best to avoid closed questions. In fact, you don't need a questionnaire at all. A brainstorming tool like AnswerGarden is ideal.

Mapping staff and student capabilities

Mapping capabilities is a separate and quite different process to mapping preferences – and it should probably follow it. Unless you know what applications to focus on, your capability assessment is liable to be too broad, leading to 'questionnaire overload.' Focus is key here: you probably don't *need* a comprehensive audit of all things digital, just some information about what learning tools are most used, are considered user-friendly and/or potentially have the greatest impact on learning. There is little point in including management tools,

How skilled would you describe yourself with each of the following? *

	Expert	Competent	Learning	Haven't used it
Google Classroom	○	○	○	○
Google Forms	○	○	○	○
Google Sites	○	○	○	○
Padlet	○	○	○	○
Trello	○	○	○	○
Quizlet	○	○	○	○
Kahoot	○	○	○	○

Figure 7.2 A Google™ form rating expertise in a range of applications.

and you need to be able to allocate questions or filter responses by subject – there's no point in knowing what English teachers think of data logging apps, and no point in knowing what maths teachers think of writing frame tools!

Capabilities are quantitative in nature, so a different kind of tool is required. You don't need to spend a fortune on expensive survey tools; either Microsoft Forms or Google Forms will do the job very nicely. To be GDPR compliant:

- Use your organisational account, not a personal one – you don't want to have student data on your own Google Drive.
- Include a suitable GDPR statement, including reference to whether you are collecting personally identifiable data (you should justify this when it is necessary – it shouldn't be in this case), what the information is to be used for and how long it will be kept.

Remember that until you've mapped your organisational preferences, you can't really construct your form, but your generic section might look something like Figure 7.2.

In order to capture subject-specific tools, you can either use branching questions or simply don't make questions compulsory so teachers of different subjects can ignore them.

Mapping and decision-making

Once you have a good idea about what applications are being used and what teachers and students think of them, you have much of the necessary information to make decisions about the ways forward. So, what else do you need to know? It is highly instructive to read some DfE documentation and see what they refer to. You might also want to see what comparable schools and colleges are doing. Based on all of this, you might realise that:

- Your digital capability is strong and that no significant change is needed to attain an acceptable minimum; you can therefore focus on more ambitious goals.
- Teachers are using a wide range of external platforms and applications in a pedagogically sound but inconsistent way, and so you need a way to centrally track learner progress and prevent data breaches. This might involve commissioning new platform(s) or learning how to make better use of what you have. There is a tricky balance to be struck here between standardising practice without stifling creativity.
- There is plenty of good practice across the organisation, but it is inconsistent and some subjects are being left behind. This can be tackled by sharing practice across teams or contracting in subject-specific training.
- There are one or more areas of specific weakness, e.g. the use of technology for assessment.
- As an organisation you are lagging behind peers and need a programme of digital refreshment. This should be carefully planned and not a knee-jerk response – see the following section on digital development planning.
- As an organisation you have gone down an idiosyncratic route and use non-standard or out-of-favour solutions. In this case you should carefully consider your options. There is much to be said for standard solutions that have readily available support and a shallow learning curve for new staff. and that inspectors will reliably recognise as good or at least standard practice. On the other hand, there is a reason why people say, 'If it ain't broke, don't fix it.' It's the learning that matters, not conformity to a norm that may or may not be optimal.

Your digital development plan

Once you know how your current digital capabilities stack up against the competition and what existing strengths and preferences in your community you can capitalise on, you are in a position to plan for the future. Typically, organisational development plans span several years, but there is a logical problem in doing this with digital learning in that the technology moves so fast that, two years in, your plan is likely to be obsolete. I have some specific suggestions for futureproofing, but the most important principles are to keep a focus on learning above all else, and to make sure you have a strong vision of where you want to be. Tech choices can be tweaked relatively painlessly as long as you keep the vision in mind. And remember, your development plan is not a Gantt chart tracking every detail of a project – it is a way to keep an eye on the big picture and track your progress.

Vision: A school where every experience is seen through a digital lens and digital solutions contribute to every aspect of student success

Mission: To apply a digital lens to every aspect of school life and use digital solutions to contribute to every aspect of student success

Issue	Obstacles	Objectives	Actions	Review dates	Modified actions
Insufficient up-to-date hardware for all students to engage in learning	Rapid obsolescence of hardware, up-front replacement cost	Source sufficient up-to-date hardware	DH Commission bids for a hardware leasing deal	End June	Extend lease deal and decommission pre-lease equipment
Changed intake means a higher number of students in tech poverty	Current systems do not allow easy loan of hardware. No way to give access outside normal hours	• Develop a hardware loan system • Provide improved access to school facilities	• LRC manager to run a hardware-load scheme • LRC manager to provide after-school access to IT facilities	End June	Employ LRC assistant
Observations reveal lack of digital learning in lessons	No culture of digital learning, highly traditional staff	Increase understanding of the benefits of digital learning	• Digital targets in all appraisals • SLT to appoint consultant to provide advice and training	April	• Extend consultant contract • Appoint ed tech champions • Ed tech interview question for all new appointments

Figure 7.3 Extract from a digital development plan including columns for obstacles, objectives, actions, review dates and modified actions.

There are a few tricks in this model of development plan designed to prevent obsolescence:

- The emphasis is on the reasons for, and obstacles to, development. These will remain relevant however much the technology landscape changes.
- Actions are followed by regular review and modified actions. Two years in, your original actions might seem quite dated, but that's fine – you can just add new actions as the landscape changes.
- There is no mention of particular hardware or software choices – these can date really fast and are not needed for this level of plan.

Understanding and planning for change

Not all change is the same, and any one-size-fits-all model of change will fail under some circumstances. Some tech changes require a tweak, others a complete overhaul. Sometimes you have the luxury of starting from scratch with time and budget; most of the time you will be responding quickly to an emerging need or the availability of a new piece of kit. I find two processes here to be helpful in understanding and managing change. The first is a very quick process suited to understanding the implications of a simple potential tech change and evaluating whether in fact to go ahead. The second is a more elaborate wraparound model that is more appropriate for planned wholescale change and requires more time and effort.

Using the SAMR model to evaluate a proposed change

SAMR (Puentedura, 2010) is a way to classify potential technical innovations according to how they impact on existing teaching and learning practices. This gives us an insight into the purposes, positives and possible negatives of making the change and allows for a more informed decision. SAMR identifies four levels of process change. Let me illustrate the first three levels with reference to four learning processes:

- Knowledge transfer from the front of a classroom
- Knowledge transfer through handouts
- Collecting in written work to assess
- Revision using flashcards

1. *Substitution*: Technology provides a like-for-like substitute for an existing process. Examples include:
    - Presenting using bullet points on PowerPoint slides instead of writing on a whiteboard.
    - Posting documents on a learning platform instead of giving out paper handouts.
    - Collecting written work using an online assignment system instead of pen and paper.
    - Posting revision flashcards online instead of on cards.
2. *Augmentation*: Technology provides a pedagogically improved version of the same process. Examples include:
    - A teacher explanation is illustrated by a YouTube video.
    - Interactive text including self-assessment questions are posted online.

- The assignment submission system allows submission of audio files as well as documents.
- Revision flashcards are adaptive, responding to what content the student knows well and less well.
3. *Modification*: Technology allows us to significantly change the task itself. Examples include:
    - Students take responsibility for a topic and produce and share podcasts.
    - Interactive tasks allow students to build their own tailored materials.
    - Students are given mark schemes, and they peer assess work using an online assignment system.
    - Score on revision tests trigger access to differentiated levels of revision flashcards.

The final level of SAMR is redefinition. It doesn't make logical sense to reference existing teaching and learning processes at this point. The essence of redefinition is to use technology to do things that simply wouldn't be possible in a conventional classroom. Examples include:

- Publishing student work on iTunes – a significant motivator
- Peer-conferencing with students in another country
- Using augmented reality to manipulate molecular structures in 3D
- Using artificial intelligence to analyse student engagement and schedule activity change

To get the most out of the SAMR model, keep two things in mind:

1. There is no hierarchy of desirability in the four levels – the 'levels' simply describe the extent to which the new technology changes existing processes. These may or may not need significant change.
2. A high level on the SAMR model does not necessarily mean cutting-edge technology – it's about the learning process.

The key to using SAMR productively is to ask slightly different questions according to the level of process change:

Substitution

1. Is there a meaningful benefit to the change?
    a. Does the change solve a problem?
    b. Does the change make a process more convenient?
2. Is there a financial cost to the change?
3. Will there be downsides to implementation?

Augmentation

1. Does the augmentation have a significant benefit for the process?
2. Assuming there is a cost, is this proportionate to the benefits for the process?
3. Are there downsides to implementation?

Table 7.1. An example of substitution

Example: Presentation software – e.g. PowerPoint, Google Slides – instead of board-writing	
1a. Does the change solve a problem?	Yes. It solves problems of illegible teacher handwriting and behaviour management as teachers face a board to write.
1b. Does the change make a process more convenient?	Yes. It makes the process of absent students catching up and quality-assuring teaching resources more convenient.
2. Is there a financial cost to the change?	If you already have an institutional office suite, e.g. for emails, then there is no additional cost.
3. Will there be downsides to implementation?	Possibly. Not all colleagues may be on board with the change, and there may be a modest increase to preparation time. Spontaneous explanation and discussion in lessons may decline.
Decision: No-brainer! There is no financial cost, and there are significant advantages to the change. Downsides are probably minor and short term. The pedagogical risks are real but can be mitigated with training.	

Table 7.2. An example of augmentation

Example: Using YouTube to augment teacher explanations	
1. Does the augmentation have a significant benefit for the process?	Yes. Video enhances explanation, making it more accessible to students.
2. Assuming there is a cost, is this proportionate to the benefits for the process?	Yes. There is no direct financial cost to YouTube use, and subscription to alternatives may also be cost-effective.
3. Are there downsides to implementation?	There are potential downsides in terms of behaviour management, but these can be mitigated, e.g. if YouTube is content-filtered and/or available only to teachers.
Decision: Another no-brainer! There is no financial cost, and there are significant advantages to the change. The behaviour management risks are real but can be mitigated.	

Table 7.3. An example of modification

Example: Adaptive revision materials	
1. Is the modified task more educationally sound than the original task?	Yes. It is a better use of revision time to focus on less well-known areas.
2. Assuming there is a cost, is this proportionate to the benefits for the process?	Yes. There are free sources of adaptive revision materials, and paid alternatives are likely to be cost-effective.
3. Are there downsides to implementation?	No. There are unlikely to be downsides.
Decision: Yet again, a no-brainer. Adaptive materials increase the efficiency of revision and can be implemented for free, with a shallow learning curve and no significant risks.	

Table 7.4. An example of redefinition

Example: Student self-publishing on iTunes	
1. Is the new task educationally sound? There are various ways in which it might be sound, but simply looking impressive is not one of them.	Publishing *per se* does not improve learning, but it might well do so indirectly if it increases student engagement. This needs careful thought.
2. Is it a good use of time, and can it be incorporated into the academic calendar?	This kind of student-centred task can be quite time-consuming. However, there are times in the academic year, e.g. after summer exams, where productivity is relatively low and little may be lost by incorporating this kind of task into teaching.
3. Are there significant downsides in terms of cost, steep learning curve or staff acceptance?	This kind of task need not be expensive, but it may require some outside-the-box thinking from teachers.
Decision: You can see that the redefinition task requires more careful thinking than the lower levels. It will come down to your judgement.	

Modification

1. Is the modified task more educationally sound than the original task?
2. Assuming there is a cost, is this proportionate to the benefits for the process?
3. Are there downsides to implementation?

Redefinition

1. Is the new task educationally sound? There are various ways in which it might be sound, but simply looking impressive is not one of them.
2. Is it a good use of time, and can it be incorporated into the academic calendar?
3. Are there significant downsides in terms of cost, steep learning curve or staff acceptance?

Co-design: a wraparound model for planning and implementing change

'Co-design' (Sanders & Stapper, 2008) means any joint activity in which developers or purchasers of a product collaborate with end users and other stakeholders on the design and/or selection of a product. In the world of digital education, co-design principles can be applied to making sure new tech tools meet the needs of an organisation and its users. JISC (2017) produced a co-design playbook (www.jisc.ac.uk/rd/how-we-innovate/co-design) to help structure involvement of end users in the whole process of technological change. The following represents a simplified version of the JISC approach.

When *co-design is appropriate*

Co-design is quite an intensive process, and it is probably overkill when purchasing a simple tool off the shelf. It comes into its own when choosing a system of major importance to students and teachers, where there is a range of available alternatives and/or these have a range of configuration options. When it comes to management information systems and Virtual Learning Environments, there is a plethora of choices, both of platforms and how to set them up. Co-design can make sense of this complexity.

> **Top tech tip**: Nothing upsets the co-design process like a default choice planted in your mind by sales folk! This is not an ideological point, just a practical one. Human decision-making is generally biased towards the default choice. If representatives of a product contact you and alert you to a need and a class of product, even if you then check out alternatives, you are likely to see them as radical alternatives to the safe default and fall back on the first option you heard about. I personally bypass this by simply refusing to speak to product representatives until I have defined the product need and reviewed options. Only at that point would I initiate contact with the representatives of the various possibilities.

Defining your end users and other stakeholders

The essence of co-design is people. Your proposed tech system might be the most impressive in the world, but it is impossible to anticipate what will grab the imagination of your end users. Consider the following:

- *Students*: This is the biggie; if your students engage with a system, everyone else will probably grow to like it. Unless it's a staff-only system, students are the most important co-designers.
- *Teachers*: Teachers are also important. They as well as students will need to engage with the system.
- *IT staff*: It's a surprisingly common scenario for managers to purchase a system and then tell their IT staff about it. That's a gamble – it *might* be fine, but equally it *might* cause huge problems – for example, if it needs to interface with your VLE or MIS and one lives on Azure and the other on AWS. It's fine, by the way, if you have no idea what any of that means; just know that it's important to check with whoever will be responsible for making it work!
- *Other stakeholders*: Consider whether anyone else needs to use the system or will receive reports generated from it.
- *Managers*: As the people that interface with students, parents, teachers, IT staff, governors, Ofsted and auditors, you probably have a good overview, so your opinion is important. However, unless it's a management system, it is likely that you will use the system less than others, so your preferences should probably fall some way down the pecking order.

Engaging with your end users

If you are serious about having end users collaborate in the selection and design of a system, then it is worth considering how you engage with them. Engagement strategies aimed at getting a group of students and/or teachers focused on the task include the following:

- *Convene a workshop*: Get interested parties together for an initial discussion
- *Host a launch event*: Whip up some excitement with food and drink
- *Elect or nominate a user panel*: Establish a group of dedicated users with some decision-making powers
- *Commission user reviews*: Ask for feedback – this need not be systematic; the aim is to engage and enthuse, not to get definitive information

- *Launch a social media group*: Involve a wider group, including those who probably would not put themselves forward for a selective group
- *Target extreme users*: Make sure the keenest and most resistant are represented

Stages of co-design

Understanding

This stage is about beginning to understand what systems exist and what others are doing, and generally to get a sense of the needs of your end users. Understanding strategies include the following:

- *Service safaris*: Jollies to other organisations to see solutions operating in a real working environment
- *Create personas*: Design profiles of composite or hypothetical students and their use of current and future technology
- *Surveys*: Use questionnaires and interviews to understand the views of end users
- *Consult experts*: At this point these should be technology-neutral
- *Immersion*: As managers, intensively use current and potential applications for a period
- *Reviews*: Find/commission reviews of current and potential solutions

Imagining

This stage is about focusing down on how you want your new system to look and behave, and anticipating and mitigating problems. Imagining strategies include the following:

- *Create a roadmap*: Plan out what features you need and how they can be obtained, e.g. integral to the product, plug-ins and bespoke developments, with a timeline
- *Imaging*: Create pictorial representations of the product, including the navigation structure and interface
- *Scenarios*: Construct sets of use-cases and check that the system can perform against them
- *Map service principles*: Make explicit the capacity a system needs (e.g. number of simultaneous users), and check these against bottlenecks (e.g. bandwidth, server memory), and what human support needs it generates

Building

The 'building' stage will look rather different according to whether you are buying an off-the-shelf system, putting together a modular system with a range of options or building something from scratch.

> **Top tech tip**: Buying an off-the-shelf product might at first glance sound rather at odds with the co-design process. But actually, it is perfectly legitimate to go through the understanding and imagining stages and make an informed decision that an off-the-shelf solution meets your needs best. That is *not* the same as simply buying a product and is much more likely to succeed.

The following are some building strategies you might try:

- *Arrange a free trial*: A free trial of a solution will allow you to fully test it, including options and plug-ins.
- *Access a prototype*: Many products do not work out of the box but require some development work before they are usable. This requires the building of a prototype, a time-consuming and potentially expensive process. However, you may be able to access an existing prototype for testing purposes.
- *Lofi-prototyping*: Sometimes you don't need a working prototype to test something – sometimes you have faith it will work on a technical level, and what you are interested in is user acceptance. A pen-and-paper sketch can accomplish that, and there are wireframing apps that allow you to mock up an application interface. An example of a wireframing application with free education accounts is Figma (www.figma.com/education/).

> **Top tech tip**: If the tech change you are planning involves replacing an existing system, it is often worth looking closely at whether you can actually achieve the change you want by updating, reconfiguring or retheming the old system. At the imagining and building stages, you may have enthusiasts and sales reps advocating for a new solution, so it may also be worth having a corresponding enthusiast or representative advocate for the potential of your old system.

Implementing and anchoring change

A technology change process does not end when you make a software decision. You need to think about training and anchoring. It is also well worth it to plan implementation in the context of the academic year. A new system that will be used by a large number of teachers and students will ideally be introduced for the start of the academic year. BUT (apologies if this is egg-sucking), if something is to go live in September, it needs to be installed, tested and staff trained before the summer break.

Training

In most industries, the norm is to spend more on training on the use of a new system than the system itself. In education there is a history of treating this kind of training as an afterthought. The message is simple: Make sure you have a suitable trainer and allocate them enough time to do a thorough job. Where at all possible, new packages should now come with a choice of video and document instructions, but for anything other than the simplest and cheapest of software, these should be an adjunct to live training rather than a substitute.

Anchoring change

This will not be news if you are an experienced manager, but most of the work managing a change is not in its implementation but in anchoring the change, i.e. making sure that there is a good level of compliance and that it becomes part of the culture of the organisation. There are a number of strategies that can help with this:

- *Policy change*: A new system will have policy implications. For example, is it mandatory? Users need to know this kind of thing if they are to comply.
- *Goal-setting*: Use of a new system lends itself well to generating appraisal targets.
- *Follow-up*: This can be by means of a range of appropriate informal and formal interactions.
- *Integration into quality improvement plans*: If a new system is to be woven into the fabric of an organisation, it may be possible to use it to address a number of quality issues. The more people that benefit in more ways, the more valued a system.
- *Incentivisation*: There are a number of ways to incentivise the use of a new digital system. One worth considering is a digital badging system. A complete badging system that includes a backlink to verify a badge online will cost a school or college a few hundred pounds a year (see, for example, Open Badges at https://openbadges.me). If you have a VLE like Moodle, you can create and award badges with a free plug-in.

Evaluating technology change

To some extent, you know whether a change in technology has worked because it just feels embedded into the culture of an organisation. However, you may want some more concrete data. During the co-design process, an important element from the management perspective is a tool's reporting ability. Generally, substantial modern software solutions should be able to produce usage reports, and I would check on this when evaluating options.

A word about decommissioning

In the excitement over your shiny new e-learning system, it is easy to forget your old system. However, there are numerous horror stories around of hasty tech change projects that have failed to consider all the functionality of an old system and that have ended up with a school or college no longer able to carry out an essential function. Here are some examples:

- Shifting from Windows devices to Chromebooks, then realising that some awarding bodies require the use of desktop software
- Shifting from Google Workspace to Office 365, then realising students can no longer make their own web pages
- Shifting from Moodle to Google Classroom, then realising you have no SCORM player and you rely on staff training materials in SCORM format

Do audit exactly what you do with any tool and make sure you have some means for continuing to do so before decommissioning anything.

Further information

In this chapter I have referred to JISC resources and models. You can read a great range of advice on digital leadership and digital change here: www.jisc.ac.uk/leadership-and-culture. For more information about the SAMR model, see Puentedura (2010), *SAMR and TPCK: Intro to advanced practice*: http://hippasus.com/resources/sweden2010/SAMR_TPCK_IntroToAdvancedPractice.pdf. See also Sanders and Stappers (2008), Co-creation and the new landscapes of design, *Co-design*, 4(1), pp. 5-18.

Glossary

Accessibility the extent to which resources and activities can be used by people with a range of abilities and preferences. Accessibility can be an important factor in student engagement, and in UK and EU Further and Higher Education, though not in schools and 6th form colleges, there is a legal requirement to comply with the EU Accessibility Directive.

Active learning this refers in a range of approaches to activities in which students take an active rather than passive role in their learning. Some approaches using the term 'active' emphasise active behaviour; for example, project work. In this book, the emphasis is on *cognitive* activity as opposed to active behaviour.

Adaptivity the real-time changing of activities or steering students to different activities, either by a teacher or software, in response to student progress. *Hard* adaptivity involves making the decision for the student, whereas *soft* adaptivity suggests a direction for the student who makes the final choice. Adaptivity can be seen as a contemporary understanding of differentiation, or alternatively as a replacement for it.

Affordances from J. J. Gibson's direct theory of perception, the relationships between a thing's capabilities and potential uses and what it looks like it can do or is for. This is an important idea in learning technology because software tends to have a wide range of potential uses but to look like it is meant to be used in a much narrower way.

Amanote a set of very well-designed free and premium annotation and note-taking tools, available as a standalone platform and as a set of VLE plug-ins. PDF documents can be annotated and stored or exported with notes. PDF worksheets can be completed and submitted online for marking.

Anchoring change the process of ensuring that new technology or tech-mediated processes are used consistently. This might involve, for example, policy change, goal-setting and incentivisation.

AnswerGarden an excellent wordcloud generator that allows you to share word entry by URL or QR code and to export completed wordclouds.

API the most common mechanism by which two platforms are integrated. Different APIs have different properties and functions; for example, they may create matching accounts across two platforms and a single sign-on to both.

Assignment a tool found in all major learning platforms that allows students to submit work for teacher assessment. Google assignments are distinguished by free plagiarism checking and quick marking made easier by pre-set comments. Moodle assignments have the most options, including the facility to record audio and video directly into the assignment and options for timing and proctoring.

Asynchronous use of technology learning activities in which communication is not in real time. For example, instructions are given to or left for students, and they work independently when they receive them. This can take place in the context of traditional face-to-face, remote or flipped learning.

Baseline assessment assessing students at the start of a key stage or learning programme in order to establish a starting point from which progress can be measured. Access to baseline assessment can carried out by online services like BKSB or put together yourself.

Blended learning learning that involves a blend of face-to-face and remote learning. Traditionally, face-to-face elements are synchronous and remote elements are asynchronous. However, this is no longer necessarily the case, as remote teaching might be by means of video meeting applications like Zoom, Teams or Meet.

Blended lessons remote lessons containing both synchronous and asynchronous elements. There are a number of blended lesson formats, varying according to the order of synchronous and asynchronous elements and the pacing of activity sequences.

BookWidgets a very well-featured commercial gamification tool that integrates with cloud office suites and VLEs. If you use a cloud office platform rather than a VLE, you have limited gamification options and BookWidgets is perhaps the tool of choice.

Bootcamp lesson a model of blended remote lesson, in which a teacher leads a class rapidly through a number of synchronous and asynchronous activities. These lessons are intensive and stressful for both teacher and students, but they represent a way to rapidly upskill students, for example before an important assessment.

Cloud-based office platforms office suites like Google for Education and Microsoft Office 365 live in the cloud and are accessed by subscription, as opposed to living on local servers. These are currently popular options for learning platforms because of their support for remote learning and industry-standard office tools. However, they provide limited education-specific functionality unless integrated with VLEs or other external platforms.

Co-design a wraparound model for planning and implementing a major technology change. It involves extended engagement with users across four stages: understanding user needs and preferences, imagining what a solution might look like and building or choosing a system.

Cognitive activation any activity that stimulates mental processing that is likely to increase learning. The classic use case for cognitive activation is starter activities, which typically involve either an exciter activity to raise interest levels, or a recap activity that leads to test-potentiation – both are forms of cognitive activation that lead to increased learning.

Cognitive load theory a theory of memory that explains how we can optimise learning by making use of the way short-term memory works. In particular, we can improve learning by reducing unnecessary demands on short-term memory (extraneous cognitive load) and increasing the uses of short-term memory that promote learning (germane cognitive load). The third kind of cognitive load, the intrinsic load of a concept or skill, cannot be altered but can be managed, for example by using animation to display an idea one part at a time.

Concept map a way to display material visually, with links connecting nodes of information. Unlike mind maps, concept maps include connections between all conceptually related information nodes. Some concept mapping software, for example XMind, has a presentation mode and can display nodes in sequence – a powerful way to present a complex idea.

Copyright a set of rights designed to protect creative material. Copyright gives you rights to control the use of your own creative material; however, it also imposes restrictions on what you can do with other people's. So, you need to be aware of what text, images and video you can publish for educational purposes without breaching copyright.

CurrikiStudio a free online platform on which you can produce H5P interactives. CurrikiStudio is unique at the time of writing in being a free online platform capable of producing H5P interactives. However, as it is hosted in the USA, it is not GDPR-compliant and should be used only to publicly share resources.

Cyberbullying using digital media to carry out bullying. Cyberbullying is extremely harmful, increasing risk of self-harm and suicidality by two to three times.

Data controller the person in an organisation responsible for maintaining data security and complying with other data protection regulations like obtaining valid consent and reporting breaches. In a school or college, this is probably not you (you should know if it is)! If you tutor privately and retain any records of your students, then you are a data controller.

Data processor anyone who works with personal data. Every time you take a register or record marks, you are processing personal data, so as a teacher, you are a data processor. As such, you need to take reasonable steps to keep this data private and secure.

DeckDeckGo an online presentation tool with a generous free tier. It is best known for its integrated polling tool and ability to embed multiple types of code from other sites. Although it is browser-based, you can edit presentations off-line.

Decommissioning the process of ceasing to use a learning platform or application. This is an essential but often neglected aspect of technology change. It is critical to list the capabilities of any system before replacing it in order to make sure that all essential functions can be performed either by the replacement system or another system within the organisation.

Diarisation recording events and responses as a form of reflective learning. Technically, this can be carried out using a range of blog, diary and journaling tools. The best of these allow students to record voice and video as well as text. Diarisation can be used for gathering evidence from placements, critical incident reflection and monitoring student engagement and mental health during periods of remote learning.

Differentiation the process of catering for students of different ability. Traditionally, differentiation has involved labelling students with an ability level and tailoring activities and resources accordingly. Generally, this has been replaced by the idea of adaptation to student progress.

Digital divide the gap in the ability to make use of digital education between those who can afford technology, in particular hardware and connectivity, and those who cannot. Although principally the result of poverty, the digital divide is sometimes complicated by chaotic family environments and lack of faith in education.

Digital natives young people who have grown up with digital technology, as opposed to older digital immigrants who have adjusted to it. The simplistic assumption that young people are inherently better with technology has been widely discredited; however, there do appear to be generational differences in attitudes and reactions to different technologies.

Discord a social media application widely used in the gaming community. Discord is an industry-standard tool and is not especially risky or insecure. However, it is a common medium through which perpetrators of various forms of online abuse contact and groom gamer victims.

Emaze a US company best known for an online presentation tool distinguished by its 3D templates. More recently, Emaze has launched a VLE platform with a modern drag-and-drop interface.

Encryption a security technique involving scrambling data so that it can be reassembled and read only by using a key. Physical devices and online connections can be encrypted, the former generally to a higher standard. Even security agencies struggle to decrypt protected hard drives.

E-safety a catchall term covering awareness of all the risks to which students are exposed when they engage in online activity. This includes content risks, conduct risks, contact risks and consumer risks.

Expertise reversal effect according to cognitive load theory, this is a phenomenon resulting from the properties of memory. When students are new to a topic, they learn most efficiently through direct instruction. However, when they have some expertise on the topic, this reverses and they get more benefit from student-centred activities.

Financial abuse controlling a victim's ability to acquire, keep or spend their own money. This is a feature of most abusive romantic relationships, but it can also be carried out by family members. In some cases it might involve an abuser running up debts

Formative assessment assessment that takes place during a programme of learning with the purpose of improving learning. Broadly, formative assessment has two purposes – to practice retrieval, and to inform both students and teachers of areas of weakness for students. Technology can help formative assessment by means of online tasks and quizzes and by providing means of responding reflectively in the form of self-assessment, goal setting and adaptive learning pathways.

Gamification the introduction of game-like characteristics to digital learning activities. Quizzes done synchronously in competition gamify the quiz experience. Timers and music make any classroom activity more game-like. Some tools, e.g. Moodle games, convert standard quizzes to games including Hangman, Snakes and Ladders, Cryptex, Crosswords and Millionaire. The general aim of gamification is to increase engagement and attention by making activities fun and congruent with digital activity outside formal education.

GDPR the EU's general data protection regulations, now enshrined in UK law as the Data Protection Act or DPA (2018). This governs what you as an individual and organisation have to do in order to protect the privacy of any data you hold on your students. The Information Commissioner's Office (ICO) can fine organisations that fail to adequately protect student data.

Generic pedagogy teaching skills and practices that are applicable across a range of subjects, as opposed to subject-specific pedagogy. The distinction was made by Shulman in the 1980s, but has recently been recognised in Ofsted documentation.

Goal setting (target setting) A motivational technique derived from Locke's goal setting theory. The idea is that knowing exactly what you want to achieve makes it easier to focus on achieving it. Most of the attention on goals has focused on SMART targets, but this has been criticised on the basis that it is unduly restrictive and makes life easier for managers rather than students.

Google Classroom a non-VLE learning platform that offers a social stream, assignment setting and tracking and integration with other Google apps like Meet. Although it lacks full VLE functionality, Classroom is extremely well designed, and it is associated with very good levels of student engagement.

Google Meet a remote meeting and teaching application. Feature access depends on subscription, but in all but the free individual accounts, Meet supports breakout rooms and polls. All versions support whiteboards. The design and user experience of Google Meet is outstanding and it is widely preferred by students and teachers to alternatives.

H5P a suite of interactive learning tools that allow teachers to create advanced learning objects such as presentations and videos with quiz questions, exportable notes, flash cards and many others. H5P plugs into VLEs and learning record stores, storing student scores. H5P can be used free in Moodle and as a desktop app called Lumi.

Humour in both presentation and assessment, whether or not the activity is mediated by technology, we have options to introduce humour. From a cognitive load perspective, understanding humour involves extraneous cognitive load, and so humour should be used sparingly. However, this needs to be balanced against the potential for improved engagement, anxiety reduction and relationship building.

Hybrid lesson a lesson in which some students are physically present and others are accessing remotely using meeting or webinar applications. Hybrid lessons pose particular challenges for teachers, because of the complexity of moving around a physical classroom and simultaneously teaching to a webcam.

Inforapid Knowledgebase an elaborate and advanced 3D mind mapping/concept mapping tool, with free online and cheap mobile app versions, that allows you to import whole documents and websites into information nodes and to create revision flashcards. This is potentially a game changer for student revision.

Information Commissioner's Office (ICO) An independent but government-funded authority set up to regulate the protection of personal data in the UK. The ICO enforces the 2018 Data Protection Act, investigating data breaches and fining organisations that are negligent in data protection.

Interactive learning any learning activities that make use of the social nature of humans by using interaction; for example whole-group debate and discussion, peer tutoring, group work, interaction with artificial intelligence, etc. This approach is associated with Lev Vygotsky's social constructivist theory.

Interactive presentation a presentation including interactive elements like quiz questions and flashcards. H5P and Quizizz have excellent interactive presentation tools, but if you don't have access to these, then interactivity can be achieved to a limited extent using conventional presentation tools like PowerPoint.

Kahoot Kahoot is best known for its well designed and highly gamified synchronous quiz platform. This was one of the first platforms to offer a truly gamified experience and to re-use public quizzes created by other users. More recently, Kahoot has diversified and offers an interactive presentation tool; however, additional tools like this are not free.

Learning Management System (LMS) See **Virtual Learning Environment (VLE)**.

Learning platform (or digital learning platform) a broad category of online platform used to support digital learning. This includes learning management systems like Moodle, but also simpler platforms like MS Teams and Google Classroom.

LearnItFast a free online tool for building adaptive revision flashcards. LearnItFast is notable for its free accounts and really fast, intuitive interface. Completed cards can be embedded in other sites.

Linear presentations presentations that proceed in a pre-set sequence, e.g. PowerPoint slides, as opposed to presentations in which the presenter can decide in what order to display items. Tools like PowerPoint and Google Slides are usually used for linear presentations. Linear presentations are the default for many teachers, but they are probably over-used. Linearity can be reduced by introducing menus and cross-slide links and by replacing multi-slide tools with zooming presenters.

Low stakes assessment formative assessment that provides opportunities to practice retrieval in a low-stress environment where results do not count towards final grades. To make assessment truly low-stakes, it is important to introduce an element of fun and not to link outcomes to working-at grades.

LTI (learning tool interoperability) a standard that allows VLEs to exchange data anonymously and allows students on one VLE to access courses and resources on another. This means that different organisations can share access to courses, and that a host VLE can sell courses to others.

Lumi a free and open-source desktop version of H5P, which can export interactives as HTML files and SCORM. This means they can be used in any VLE and any browser without a VLE. The limitation of HTML files is that they are not linked to a system that can retain scores; however, they are still useful where there is VLE access.

Microlearning the practice of pushing out small chunks of information or small assessment tasks by digital means to students as a way to 'dripfeed' learning. Short sections of text or a question or other interactive (or links to it) are sent to students, usually in a mobile-friendly form so that they can be processed with minimal effort.

Mindmap a way to present material visually. This differs from a concept map in that information nodes are hierarchical, moving out from the centre and divided. No links are possible between parallel nodes. This structure reflects Tony Buzan's theory of knowledge.

Moodle globally the most popular and arguably the most powerful Virtual Learning Environment platform. In recent years Moodle has lost ground to heavily marketed commercial VLEs and, more recently, cloud-based office suites. Although it requires some building by a Learning Technologist, a well-designed Moodle still offers the most versatile range of learning experiences.

Moodle Timeline a Moodle course format that presents posts and activities in a social stream. This was developed as a response to the growing popularity of social learning platforms like Google Classroom or Microsoft Teams. It effectively replaces the old Moodle social format.

MS Teams an integrated communications system, part of the Office 365 suite. Teams comprises a structured social stream and a remote meeting tool, both with access to group and individual messaging. There is also an assignment system and the ability to integrate with external applications. Teams is currently popular as a learning platform, but has been criticised for its design and lack of education functionality.

Multimedia communication using a range of information formats, including text, images, audio and video. It is widely believed that presenting in multimedia has the potential to enhance learning; however, designing multimedia resources is not a straightforward task, as additional media can easily overload short term memory capacity.

NANNI (nude and nearly nude images) the preferred term amongst the authorities for the kinds of erotic-intended images shared in sexting. Sharing NANNIs is now a normal part of many people's romantic relationships; however, it leaves participants open to later sextortion and revenge porn.

Nearpod a popular external learning platform that allows you to quickly build lessons by means of sequencing presentations, simple quizzes, polls, PDFs and collaborative spaces. It also allows you to access a huge range of shared resources, most mapped on to the US curriculum. Nearpod has European servers and hence it is GDPR compliant, and it integrates into a good range of base learning platforms.

Office 365 Microsoft's leading cloud office system. This includes OneDrive file storage, Outlook email and online versions of office software like Word, PowerPoint and Excel. Recently the Teams communication system was added, this being Microsoft's answer to Google Classroom and representing Microsoft's attempt to go head-to-head with Google and older VLE systems.

Ofsted the Office for Standards in Education, the government inspectorate for schools and colleges in England and Wales since the 1990s. Before this, inspection was carried out by local authorities. Ofsted are controversial because their brief, unlike that of the old LEA inspectors, is primarily to judge rather than support.

Personalisation all the ways in which we can tailor an individual's learning experience to their needs and preferences. This includes meeting accessibility needs, adapting to student progress and generally offering options where possible. These may be pedagogical, for example in student-led goal setting, or visual, for example in the ability to choose a light or dark site theme.

Podcast a set of voice or video recordings that are released according to a schedule. In digital learning, podcasts are typically short recordings put together by teachers and regularly pushed out to students. This is an example of microlearning.

PowerPoint Microsoft's presentation tool. PowerPoint has been part of Microsoft's Office Suite since the 1990s. It is probably the most popular presentation tool in education and other industries. Currently, PowerPoint is very much standard practice, as the norm is to base a lesson structure around a presentation, thus demonstrating lesson planning in the absence of a written lesson plan. However, the affordances of PowerPoint have been heavily criticised, and there is a range of alternative presentation tools.

Prevent the UK government's approach to disrupting and preventing radicalisation. Schools and colleges have an obligation to engage with the Prevent programme. In its early days Prevent caused controversy by its focus on young Muslims; however, the current programme is more sophisticated and focuses on a range of political and religious groups and issues.

Quizlet a popular free site and mobile app for creating and sharing revision cards.

Radicalisation the process in which a person is manipulated to come to support and perhaps participate in an extremist ideology. This may lead to involvement in terrorism.

SAMR a model of technology change in which new technologies are classified according to the extent of change they will bring about in existing processes. These extents are important because they affect the criteria for deciding whether to adopt the applications.

SCORM stands for Shareable Content Object Reference Model: SCORM is a set of standards for sharing content between VLEs. A SCORM package is created using specialist development software and displayed in a VLE. Engagement and scores are passed to the VLE's records. Traditionally, SCORM has been the main way to produce interactive learning objects, but it was always limited by the requirement for a hosting VLE. There is currently a debate about the extent to which SCORM can be replaced by H5P.

Screen recording recording what happens on your screen as a video. This is used most often for creating 'how-to' videos and for recording asynchronous presentations. The most sophisticated screen recording tools are desktop-based, e.g. Open Broadcast Studio (OBS); however, there are also convenient online tools like Story Express. These generally allow you to record yourself (audio or video) narrating what is happening on screen.

Scroll of death the old-fashioned default view for a VLE course, in which resources and activities were aligned in a single long list, ordered by topic or week. This is no longer common practice, but it was such a poor design that for many it still defines the VLE experience and has contributed to negative perceptions of the VLE model.

Self-assessment Systematically judging your mastery of course elements. Typically, this might be against every assessment criterion or learning outcome. Responses can be binary (yes, no) or by means of a Likert scale or semantic differential. Technically, self-assessment can be carried out using any form technology.

Self-determination theory a theory of motivation based on the idea that people seek autonomy, competence and social relationships. The more that our work practices, including digital learning, can satisfy these needs, the harder we work at them. The major application in digital education is in motivating teachers by allowing them a degree of choice in their use of learning technology and fostering their beliefs about their competence in using it.

Seneca Learning a small but influential company specialising in advanced solutions for digital education. They are best known for their generous free access to a large selection of interactives mapped on to the England and Wales curriculum. Paid organisational accounts give access to advanced analytics and advanced modes that point students towards particular activities according to their individual progress and upcoming assessments.

Sexting See **NANNIs**.

Sexual exploitation online the deliberate exploitation of young or otherwise vulnerable people. This usually begins with grooming, then, when the perpetrator has gained their trust, progresses to persuasion or coercion to either meet in person for sexual contact or engage in online sexual activity.

Slides.com an online presentation tool best known for its ability to embed other websites and present them. This makes Slides a particularly good tool for delivering training on online learning tools as slides of information can be interspersed with live demonstrations in the same presentation.

Sticky notes a number of sites allow posting of digital notes designed to simulate the experience of posting physical sticky notes onto some kind of board. These lend themselves to brainstorming and to sorting tasks. A limitation of most sites is that students are anonymous, but modern VLEs like Moodle now support stickies.

Subject-specific pedagogy as distinct from generic pedagogy, subject-specific pedagogy involves teaching skills and practices that are associated with a single subject or a smaller group of subjects. Digital examples of subject-specific pedagogy include the use of data loggers in science and writing frames in English.

Summary builder an H5P tool that allows users to build summaries of a topic by selecting from multiple-choice answers. This summary is equivalent to the summary section at the end of an article or chapter, but the building process is better because it generates a higher level of germane cognitive load than simply reading.

Summative assessment assessments that aim to measure a student's learning after learning has taken place. This can be by means of terminal exams, unit tests and portfolios. Technology can support summative assessments through online assignment marking, e-portfolios and online exams. Preparation for exams can be achieved through online quizzes and adaptive flashcards.

Synchronous use of technology conducting learning activities in real time, for example through remote meeting applications. Other synchronous tools include instant messaging apps and live quizzes like Kahoot. Synchronous apps can be used in the physical classroom and remote lessons.

Technology-enhanced learning a very broad term meaning any form of learning that makes use of digital technology. This includes online and desktops apps supporting synchronous and asynchronous activity during conventional, blended and remote learning.

True-or-false questions the simplest form of formative assessment, and very easy to create using learning technology. True-or-false has its place but should probably be used sparingly because it results in less germane cognitive load than other question formats.

Virtual Learning Environment (VLE) a content management system with education-specific features and multiple layers of access so that managers, teachers and students can access different areas and carry out different tasks. Once repositories of files, modern VLEs support remote teaching and multiple synchronous and asynchronous activities. They are the most versatile and powerful learning platforms; however, they have a steeper learning curve than simpler systems like Google Classroom and require more building, maintenance and onboarding.

Walled garden a self-contained learning platform that is not combined or integrated with other tools. This is now a dated idea, and most platforms can be made to integrate to a greater or lesser extent with others. No single platform provides an optimum experience across the board, so some degree of integration is generally considered desirable.

Webinar literally an online seminar. A model of online teaching and learning in which students watch a teacher presentation without the facility to interact or for the teacher to see them. The webinar approach is used for online training delivered to very large groups, in which the numbers make interaction impractical. It has also been recommended in situations where students do not wish to display their face or surroundings.

Whiteboard this can be physical – in the face-to-face classroom - or virtual. Physical interactive whiteboards have now largely been replaced by touchscreens, as the latter have better resolution and brightness. Virtual whiteboards can be used in remote lessons or indeed face-to-face lessons with some kind of touchpad, such as a tablet. Of the free whiteboards, I recommend Google Jamboard.

Wordcloud a visual way to display words on a screen, for example from a brainstorm or pasted from a document. The frequency of each input word is represented by its size. This gives an indication of the popularity of each word.

YouTube the best-known video streaming service. You can create a free individual or institutional account and curate videos there for sharing. You can also make videos in YouTube and live stream. YouTube videos can be embedded in other sites and interactive video tools like H5P.

Zoom a remote teaching application that can be used for remote teaching. Zoom provides a generous individual account but institutional accounts are more than expensive than alternatives. Although Zoom is not now any less secure than alternatives like MS Teams or Google Meet, it has been a particular target for hackers, and hacker access to remote lessons – 'zoom-bombing' – has been a problem for teachers.

Zooming presenters presentations tools like Prezi and Focuski, which zoom in and out of a large canvas. This means that they afford non-linear presentations and come into their own when you want to move spontaneously between content in order to support a free-flowing discussion.

Appendix
Brief accessibility audit

Sampling pages

Your sample of web pages and other material needs to include:

- Your homepage
- Pages that are mostly text based
- Pages including images, video and audio content (if you use them)
- Pages with interactive tools, e.g. forms
- The login page
- Downloadable documents, e.g. PDFs and Word documents
- Pages with pop-up windows (if you use them)
- Navigation pages, including your sitemap and search tools (if you use these)
- Pages with key information and tools, e.g. accessibility information and privacy policy

How to check pages

The following page provides information about how to judge whether these criteria are met: https://www.gov.uk/government/publications/doing-a-basic-accessibility-check-if-you-cant-do-a-detailed-one/doing-a-basic-accessibility-check-if-you-cant-do-a-detailed-one.

You should complete the following form for each sampled page

You may use the principle of common sense when carrying out the audit. For example, if you have a spelling test where the words are presented as audio, it would be illogical to provide a textual caption.

Page title:

Criterion	Plain English Explanation	Outcome
Text accessibility		
Are heading levels styled properly?	Headings should have proper heading levels, not just be bold or enlarged	Pass [ ] Fail [ ] N/A [ ]
Do pages work when styles are disabled?	Pages should be usable without styling such as font size and colour.	Pass [ ] Fail [ ] N/A [ ]
Do instructions rely on visual cues?	Instructions for using a page should not rely on visual cues, e.g. 'the blue button'	Pass [ ] Fail [ ] N/A [ ]
Are the words over links descriptive?	Wording of links should be descriptive, e.g. 'click to answer' rather than 'click here'	Pass [ ] Fail [ ] N/A [ ]
Do pages have descriptive titles?	Pages should have descriptive titles so that users making use of search tools can find them	Pass [ ] Fail [ ] N/A [ ]
Multimedia accessibility		
Do images have an alt text description?	Non-decorative images should have a text description to make sense to visually impaired users	Pass [ ] Fail [ ] N/A [ ]
Do video and audio have captions?	Video and audio should have captions so that hearing-impaired users can follow	Pass [ ] Fail [ ] N/A [ ]
Does audio/video have a description?	If sounds in a video/audio are unexplained by transcript/captions they need a separate description	Pass [ ] Fail [ ] N/A [ ]
Is text embedded in images?	Text may not be visible only in the form of an image, as it will be invisible to text reader technology	Pass [ ] Fail [ ] N/A [ ]
Interactive tools accessibility		
Are form fields marked up properly?	Form fields must be marked up as fields so that text readers will identify them	Pass [ ] Fail [ ] N/A [ ]
Are form fields labelled properly?	It should be obvious from form labels what information is required	Pass [ ] Fail [ ] N/A [ ]
Are form field labels consistent?	Labelling equivalent fields differently on different pages causes unnecessary confusion	Pass [ ] Fail [ ] N/A [ ]
Do users get a warning before timing out?	It must be clear to a user with sensory impairments when they are going to be logged out	Pass [ ] Fail [ ] N/A [ ]
Are error messages transparent to users?	Error messages should explain why a form field has not been completed correctly	Pass [ ] Fail [ ] N/A [ ]
Can users check answers before submitting?	This is most important where a contract is being agreed. You can select N/A for education forms	Pass [ ] Fail [ ] N/A [ ]
Do form elements work as expected?	Form elements should not do odd things like take you to an unrelated page when selected	Pass [ ] Fail [ ] N/A [ ]
Document accessibility NB non-essential documents published before September 2018 are exempt		
Do documents have descriptive titles?	It must be clear to someone searching for a document what it is for	Pass [ ] Fail [ ] N/A [ ]
Are heading levels styled properly?	Headings should have proper heading levels, not just be bold or enlarged	Pass [ ] Fail [ ] N/A [ ]
Do instructions rely on visual cues?	Instructions for using a page should not rely on visual cues e.g. 'the blue button'	Pass [ ] Fail [ ] N/A [ ]
Are the words over links descriptive?	Wording of links should be descriptive e.g. 'click to answer' rather than 'click here'	Pass [ ] Fail [ ] N/A [ ]
Do images have an alt text description?	Non-decorative images should have a text description to make sense to visually impaired users	Pass [ ] Fail [ ] N/A [ ]

(Continued)

Page title:

Criterion	Plain English Explanation	Outcome
Accessibility across devices		
Do pages respond to a phone or tablet change of orientation?	If you view your page on a tablet or phone, does it still work when you change orientation?	Pass [ ] Fail [ ] N/A [ ]
Does single finger navigation work?	For users with impaired dexterity, the site should be navigable on a phone or tablet with one finger	Pass [ ] Fail [ ] N/A [ ]
Does the page require complex motions?	You should not need to shake or tilt a device to make full use of the page on a mobile device	Pass [ ] Fail [ ] N/A [ ]
Keyboard-only access		
Can the page be navigated with a keyboard?	It must be possible to tab through a page or use up and down keys, and not need a mouse	Pass [ ] Fail [ ] N/A [ ]
Can you see where you are on a page?	If you tab through a page, you should be able to tell where you are	Pass [ ] Fail [ ] N/A [ ]
Does the tab order make sense?	When you tab through a page, the order in which you arrive at each section should make sense	Pass [ ] Fail [ ] N/A [ ]
Does anything weird happen when tabbing?	You should be able to tab through a page without anything unexpected happening, e.g. changing the page	Pass [ ] Fail [ ] N/A [ ]
Do you get stuck when tabbing?	You should be able to tab right through a page without getting stuck on a page element	Pass [ ] Fail [ ] N/A [ ]
Are forms usable without a mouse?	You should be able to tab between form fields and to the submit button	Pass [ ] Fail [ ] N/A [ ]
Can you tab directly to page content?	There should be a way to get quickly to the main content on a page	Pass [ ] Fail [ ] N/A [ ]
Zooming and magnifying		
Is content usable when text is enlarged?	You should be able to enlarge the text without any weirdness	Pass [ ] Fail [ ] N/A [ ]
Is content usable when you zoom in?	You should be able to zoom into part of a page without any weirdness	Pass [ ] Fail [ ] N/A [ ]
Is there sufficient text-background contrast?	There should be sufficient contrast for users with mild visual impairments to see text clearly	Pass [ ] Fail [ ] N/A [ ]
Is the contrast on buttons sufficient?	There should be sufficient contrast for users with mild visual impairments to use buttons	Pass [ ] Fail [ ] N/A [ ]
Interactive and flashing content		
Can moving or flashing content be disabled?	You should be able to disable distracting content	Pass [ ] Fail [ ] N/A [ ]
Is there autoplay audio or video?	Ideally there should not be autoplay content. If there is, it is essential that it is easy to stop it	Pass [ ] Fail [ ] N/A [ ]
Is there an alternative to map content?	There should always be an alternative way to find locations where there is a map	Pass [ ] Fail [ ] N/A [ ]
Searching and navigation		
Is there more than one way to navigate?	There should be at least two ways – for example, search bar, site map, category links, breadcrumbs	Pass [ ] Fail [ ] N/A [ ]
Is navigation consistent across the site?	Navigation aids like breadcrumbs and searches should work consistently	Pass [ ] Fail [ ] N/A [ ]
Do links respond correctly to mouse clicks?	Links should activate when a mouse button is released, not on hover or down-click	Pass [ ] Fail [ ] N/A [ ]

(Continued)

(Continued)

Page title:		
Criterion	**Plain English Explanation**	**Outcome**
Page code		
Are tables and bulleted lists coded properly?	This is important so that assistive technology can make sense of the content	Pass [ ] Fail [ ] N/A [ ]
Does the code include the language?	The page code should include 'en' or 'gb' so that assistive technology knows the language to read in	Pass [ ] Fail [ ] N/A [ ]
Do media players have proper buttons?	The code for buttons should include informative terms like 'play,' as assistive tech will pick this up	Pass [ ] Fail [ ] N/A [ ]

Index

Accessibility 6, 23, 25, 43, 67, 80, 83–86, 113
Active learning 5, 6, 9, 48, 98, 113
Adaptivity 6, 29, 31, 34–36, 113
Affordances 7, 11, 12, 15, 58, 68, 98, 99, 113
Amanote 42, 57, 113
Anchoring change 110–111, 113
Animation 13
AnswerGarden 57, 100, 113
API 48, 113
Assignment 12, 30, 39, 42, 48, 51, 52, 56, 97, 104, 105, 114
Asynchronous use of technology 1, 3, 6, 22, 23, 60–62, 76, 114
Audio 9, 11, 12, 20, 22, 23–25

Base platforms 48, 52, 53
Baseline assessment 30–32, 114
Blended learning 3, 4, 28, 36, 60, 114
Blended lessons 60, 62, 114
BookWidgets 43–44, 114
Bullet points 2, 7, 12, 13, 68

Canvas (VLE) 44, 53, 68, 99
Cloud-based office platforms 48–52, 114
Co-design 106–110, 114
Cognitive activation 5, 12, 16, 25, 114
Cognitive load 8–9, 12, 13, 14, 16, 20, 22, 23, 25, 33, 63, 83, 114
Concept map 19, 44, 115
Copyright 86–87, 115
CurrikiStudio 18, 74, 115
Cyberbullying 89–90, 115

Data controller 81, 115
Data processor 81, 115
DeckDeckGo 20, 115

Decommissioning 111, 115
Diarisation 36–37, 115
Differentiation see adaptation
Digital divide 4, 116
Digital leadership 96–98
Digital natives 2, 116
DPA 80

E-books 25–28
Emaze 19, 116
E-safety 87–94, 116
Expertise reversal effect 9, 116
Extraneous cognitive load 9, 12, 14, 16, 22, 23, 33, 115

Financial abuse & exploitation 91–92, 116
Flashcards 29, 44, 45, 57, 104, 117
Flipped lessons 3, 4, 19, 28, 42, 57, 62, 114
Focuski 16
Formative assessment 29, 30, 32–39, 43, 116

Gamification 29, 38, 42–44, 114, 117
GDPR 19, 80, 81, 82, 83, 101, 117
Generic pedagogy 117
Germane cognitive load 9, 20, 115
Goal setting (target setting) 34–35, 117
Google Assignment 42
Google Classroom 4, 12, 19, 42, 43, 49–50, 51, 52, 53, 54, 58, 70, 77, 101, 111, 117
Google Forms 21, 30, 31, 32, 34, 36, 38, 101
Google Meet 3, 53, 63, 65, 66, 83, 117
Google schools 8
Google Slides 11, 12, 15, 20, 71

H5P 11, 18–19, 21, 22, 24, 25, 27, 38, 39, 49, 45, 74, 117
Humour 33, 117

Hybrid classroom 3, 39, 78, 117
Hybrid lesson 117

Information Commissioner's Office (ICO) 83, 117
Interactive learning 5, 6, 11, 15, 18, 21, 25, 26, 38, 63, 72, 98, 118
Interactive book 25–26
Interactive presentation 14, 15, 18–19, 20, 24, 25, 118
Interactive video 21, 23
Intrinsic cognitive load 9, 12, 14
Intrinsic motivation 8

Kahoot 38, 74, 118

Learning Management System (LMS) See Virtual Learning Environment (VLE)
Learning platform (or digital learning platform) 8, 19, 26, 30, 33, 34, 38, 43, 47–59, 63, 65, 68, 74, 77, 81, 85, 86, 87, 102, 104, 107, 113, 118
LearnItFast 45, 46, 57, 118
Linear presentations 11–12, 19, 118
Lockdown 1, 76
Low stakes assessment 32, 118
LTI (learning tool interoperability) 53, 118
Lumi 11, 18–19, 21, 27, 117, 118

Mapping technology use 98–100
Memorable learning 5
Microlearning 58, 118
Mindmap 19, 33, 119
Miro 20, 45
Moodle 2, 7, 12, 19, 25, 34, 35, 37, 38, 42, 44, 50, 53–58, 119
MS Teams 3, 12, 19, 38, 43, 50–51, 52, 53, 66–67, 68, 70, 71, 72, 73, 74, 77, 79, 81, 86, 118
Multimedia 11, 20–27, 39, 51, 119

NANNI (nude and nearly nude images) 90–91, 119
Nearpod 15, 52, 53, 60, 74, 119

OBS 22
Office 365 19, 100, 119
Ofsted 5, 8, 108, 119

Personalisation 6, 119–120
Podcast 11, 25, 105, 120
PowerPoint 2, 7, 11–16, 68, 70, 71, 104, 106, 120
Prevent 120
Prezi 16–17

Quizzizz 15

Remote digital teaching 3, 60–79
Retrieval practice 32–33

SAMR model of change 104–106, 120
SCORM 19, 53, 111, 120
Screen recording 21–22
Scroll of death 7, 54, 58, 68, 120
Self-assessment 34, 120
Self-determination theory 7, 8, 98, 121
Seneca Learning 53, 121
Sexting see NANNIs
Sexual exploitation online 91, 121
Slides.com 20, 121
Sticky notes 121
Structure strip 46
Subject-specific pedagogy 30, 57, 101
Summary builder 121
Summative assessment 121
Synchronous 1, 3, 6, 12, 30, 38, 60–61, 76, 114, 121

Teaching assistant 77–78
True-or-false questions 9, 33, 38, 39, 122

Video 11, 13, 19, 20–24, 36, 47, 62, 71, 74, 76, 81, 85, 86, 87, 104, 114
Virtual Learning Environment (VLE) 2, 12, 19, 53–58, 68, 122

Walled garden 48, 122
Webinar 63, 122
Whiteboard 71–72, 122
Wordcloud 122

YouTube 20, 122

Zoom 7, 50, 53, 63, 68, 73, 74, 77, 82, 86, 122
Zooming presenters 16–18, 122

For Product Safety Concerns and Information please contact our EU representative GPSR@taylorandfrancis.com
Taylor & Francis Verlag GmbH, Kaufingerstraße 24, 80331 München, Germany

www.ingramcontent.com/pod-product-compliance
Lightning Source LLC
Chambersburg PA
CBHW080225170426
43192CB00015B/2758